PENGUIN BOOKS

HOW NOT TO WRITE A NOVEL

ABOUT THE AUTHORS

Howard Mittelmark is the author of the novel *Age of Consent*; as a ghostwriter/collaborator, he has had a hand in dozens of novels and memoirs, including two *New York Times* bestsellers. He has worked for literary agencies, and publishers of both books and magazines, in various editorial capacities. His book reviews and essays have appeared in *The New York Times*, *The Washington Post*, *The Philadelphia Inquirer*, *The International Herald-Tribune*, *Hollywood Reporter*, and other publications.

To correspond or find out more, visit www.howardmittelmark.com

Sandra Newman is the author of two novels, *Cake* and *The Only Good Thing Anyone Has Ever Done* (a finalist for the *Guardian* First Book Award). Her memoir, *Folk Tales of the Rich*, is forthcoming from Random House next year. She has taught fiction at Temple University, Chapman University, the University of Colorado, the Unterberg Poetry Center, and Gotham Writers' Workshop. Her fiction, essays, talks, and reviews have appeared in *Harper's*, *Conjunctions*, *Salmagundi*, the *Observer* and *Express* newspapers, in Granta's *Family Wanted*, and on BBC Radio 3 and 4.

To correspond or find out more, visit www.sandranewman.org

D1146669

HOW *not* to WRITE a NOVEL

200 Mistakes To Avoid At All Costs If
You Ever Want To Get Published

HOWARD MITTELMARK
and SANDRA NEWMAN

PENGUIN BOOKS

PENGUIN BOOKS

Published by the Penguin Group

Penguin Books Ltd, 80 Strand, London WC2R 0RL, England

Penguin Group (USA) Inc., 375 Hudson Street, New York, New York 10014, USA

Penguin Group (Canada), 90 Eglinton Avenue East, Suite 700, Toronto, Ontario, Canada M4P 2Y3

(a division of Pearson Penguin Canada Inc.)

Penguin Ireland, 25 St Stephen's Green, Dublin 2, Ireland (a division of Penguin Books Ltd)

Penguin Group (Australia), 250 Camberwell Road, Camberwell, Victoria 3124, Australia

(a division of Pearson Australia Group Pty Ltd)

Penguin Books India Pvt Ltd, 11 Community Centre, Panchsheel Park, New Delhi – 110 017, India

Penguin Group (NZ), 67 Apollo Drive, Rosedale, North Shore 0632, New Zealand

(a division of Pearson New Zealand Ltd)

Penguin Books (South Africa) (Pty) Ltd, 24 Sturdee Avenue, Rosebank, Johannesburg 2196, South Africa

Penguin Books Ltd, Registered Offices: 80 Strand, London WC2R 0RL, England

www.penguin.com

First published in the United States by HarperCollins 2008
First published in Great Britain by Penguin Books 2009

010

Designed by Kara Strubel
Printed in England by Clays Ltd, St Ives plc

ISBN: 978-0-141-03854-4

www.greenpenguin.co.uk

MIX
Paper from
responsible sources
FSC™ C018179
www.fsc.org

Penguin Books is committed to a sustainable
future for our business, our readers and our planet.
This book is made from Forest Stewardship
Council™ certified paper.

CONTENTS

INTRODUCTION

———

Unpublished authors often cite the case of John Kennedy Toole, who, unable to find a publisher for his novel, *A Confederacy of Dunces*, took his own life. Thereafter, his mother relentlessly championed the book, which was eventually published to great acclaim and earned him a posthumous Pulitzer Prize for fiction.

Yes, we say, that is a strategy, but it is a strategy that demands a remarkable level of commitment from the author's mother, and an even greater commitment from the author. And, of course, it puts a serious crimp in the book tour. But even more to the point, it will work only if you have in fact written a masterpiece that awaits only the further enlightenment of the publishing industry and the reading public to receive the treatment it deserves.

If this is the case, we are no good to you. If there is, however, any chance that your writing could stand some improvement, we can help.

Unpublished novelists can, of course, turn to the innumerable books on writing already available: magisterial tomes from great authors; arc-schemes and plot-generating formulas from less-great authors; inspirational books about releasing the inner artist or freeing the creative mind.

We do not discourage you from reading any of them. The best are themselves good writing, and the more good writing you read, the better a writer you might become. Inspirational books might indeed inspire you, or at least serve as Dumbo's magic feather. Even plot wheels are good for a laugh, and you can always while away a merry hour putting together new characters from the Big Box o' Traits like a Mr. Potato Head, and then return to writing your novel refreshed and renewed.

But if reading Stephen King on writing really did the trick, we would all by now be writing engrossing vernacular novels that got on the bestseller lists; and it has been demonstrated through years of workshops that the Artist Within tends to make the same mistakes as the artist within everybody else. Furthermore, in trying to write novels to the specifications of a manual, the writer will often feel that her voice and imagination are being stifled, and nobody can fail to notice that for every "rule" of writing these books present, novels can be found in which it has been broken with great success.

Therefore we saw a need, a service we could provide.

All these many writing books strive to offer distinct, sometimes radically different approaches to writing a novel. But if you locked all their authors in a room and slowly started filling it with water, and the only way they could escape was to reach some consensus on writing, their only hope for survival would be to agree on the things you *shouldn't* do—which is to say, the contents of *How Not to Write a Novel.*

We do not presume to tell you how or what to write. We are merely telling you the things that editors are too busy rejecting your novel to tell you themselves, pointing out the mistakes they recognize instantly because they see them again and again in novels they do not buy.

We do not propose any rules; we offer observations. "No right on red" is a rule. "Driving at high speed toward a brick wall usually ends badly" is an observation.

Hundreds of unpublished and unpublishable novels have passed across our desks, so we have been standing here by the side of the road for a very long time. Had you been standing here with us, you would have seen the same preventable tragedies occurring over and over, and you would have made the same observations.

Do not think of us as traffic cops, or even driving instructors. Think of us instead as your onboard navigation system, available day or night, a friendly voice to turn to whenever you look up, lost and afraid, and think "How the fuck did I end up here?"

PART I

—

PLOT

Not just a bunch of stuff that happens

As a writer you have only one job: to make the reader turn the page. Of all the tools a writer uses to make a reader turn the page, the most essential is the plot. It doesn't matter if the plot is emotional ("Will Jack's fear of commitment prevent him from finding true love with Synthya?"), intellectual ("But Jack, Synthya's corpse was found in a locked room, with nothing but a puddle on the floor next to her and a recently thawed leg of mutton on the end table!"), or physical ("Will Jack's unconstitutional torture of Synthya Abu Dhabi, the international terrorist, lead to the location of the ticking bomb?") as long as it compels the reader to find out what happens next. If your reader doesn't care what happens next—it doesn't.

Typically, the plot of a *good* novel begins by introducing a sympathetic character who wrestles with a thorny problem. As the plot thickens, the character strains every resource to solve the problem, while shocking developments and startling new information help or hinder her on the way. Painful inner conflicts drive her onward but sometimes also paralyze her at a moment of truth. She finally overcomes the problem in a way that takes the reader totally by surprise, but in retrospect seems both elegant and inevitable.

The plot of a typical *unpublished* novel introduces a protagonist, then introduces her mother, father, three brothers, and her cat, giving each a long scene in which they exhibit their typical behaviors one after another. This is followed by scenes in which they interact with each other in different combinations, meanwhile driving restlessly to restaurants, bars, and each other's homes, all of which is described in detail.

A typical plot event in an unpublished novel is when the protagonist gets a disastrous haircut, at a moment when her self-esteem is hanging *by threads*. This sets the character up for the ensuing "Mother thinks protagonist spends too much on haircuts, but is made to see that self-esteem is crucial to mental health" scene, the "boyfriend doesn't understand character's needs, but finally acknowledges the gendered basis of his priorities," scene, and the "taking a bubble bath to relax after stress-filled scenes" scene, in which the protagonist mentally recapitulates the previous three scenes. Cue waking up the next morning on page 120, with anything resembling a story yet to appear on the horizon.

Sometimes a contemplative prologue will depict the protagonist looking out the window and thinking of all the philosophical conundrums the author will not have time to present in the ensuing narrative. Sometimes the prologue simply presents those philosophical conundrums in a voice that issues from nowhere. Sometimes the prologue dispenses with philosophy completely and presents a protagonist looking out the window thinking about hair products.

A great many plot problems that show up in unpublished manuscripts can be resolved with a single strategy. *Know* what the chase is, and cut to it. Do not write hundreds of pages without knowing what story you really want to tell. Do not write hundreds of pages explaining why you want to tell the story you are about to tell, why the characters are living the way they are when the story begins, or what past events made the characters into people who would have that story. Write hundreds of pages *of* the story, or else you'll find that what you write will not be shelved in the libraries of the future but will instead form the landfill upon which those libraries are built. In fact, employing any of the plot mistakes that follow will guarantee that your novel will be only a brief detour in a ream of paper's journey to mulch.

1

BEGINNINGS AND SETUPS

A manuscript comes screaming across the sky . . .

Many writers kill their plots in their infancy with an ill-conceived premise or an unreadable opening. Try any of the strategies we've collected in our extensive field work, and you too can cut off narrative momentum at the ankles.

The Lost Sock

Where the plot is too slight

"Fools," Thomas Abrams thought, shaking his head as he completed his inspection of the drainage assembly under the worried eyes of Len Stewart. "Foolish, foolish, fools," he muttered. Squirming out from under the catchment basin, he stood up and brushed off the grit that clung to his gray overalls. Then he picked up his clipboard and made a few notes on the form, while Len waited anxiously for the verdict. Thomas didn't mind making him wait.

"Well," he said, as he finished and put the pen away. "Well, well, well."

"What is it?" Len asked, unable to keep a tremor out of his voice.

"When will you people learn that you can't use a B-142 joint-enclosure with a 1811-D nipple cinch?"

"B-but—" Len stammered.

"Or maybe, let me take a wild guess here, just maybe, you confused an 1811-D with an 1811-E?" He paused to let it sink in before delivering the death-blow. " . . . *Again.*"

He left Len speechless and walked away without a look back, chuckling ruefully as he imagined the look on Len's face when he fully realized the implications of his mistake.

Here the main conflict is barely adequate to sustain a *Partridge Family* episode. Remember that this drama has to carry the reader through 300-odd pages. The central dilemma of a novel should be important enough to change someone's life forever.

Furthermore, it should be something of *broad* interest. One of the first stumbling blocks a novelist must overcome is the misapprehension that what is of interest to him will necessarily be of interest to anybody else. A novel is *never* an opportunity to vent about the things that your roommates, friends, or mother cannot bear to listen to one more time. No matter how passionate and just your desire to see the masculine charms of the short man appreciated by the fair sex, or to excoriate landlords who refuse to make plumbing repairs, even when in violation of the specific wording of the lease, which wording he might pretend to be unaware of, but you know better because you have made highlighted copies for him as well as for your roommates, friends, and mother—these are not plots but gripes.

This is not to say that a short man, unlucky in love and living in a house with substandard plumbing, cannot be your hero, but his height and plumbing should be background and texture, sketched in briefly as he heads to the scene of the crime, wondering how the hell anyone could get injuries like that from a leg of mutton.

The Waiting Room

In which the story is too long delayed

Reggie boarded the train at Montauk and found a seat near the dining car. As he sat there, smelling the appalling cheeseburgers from the adjoining carriage, he started thinking about how he had decided to become a doctor. Even as a boy, he had been interested in grotesque diseases. But did that mean he had a vocation? The train jolted, keeping him from falling asleep, and the smell of those cheeseburgers was making him nauseous. It was the same way the sight of blood still made him feel, he realized. Why had he made that decision, so many years ago?

Montauk rushed backward in the windows . . .

(10 pages later:)

The last houses of Montauk were tiny among the sandy grass. They seemed to shine against the backdrop of Reggie's continuing gloom as he considered further the reasons for his current predicament. If only he had done the biology PhD he'd originally wanted, instead of taking the advice of Uncle Frank. Uncle Frank had said to him on that occasion, scratching his hairy neck as was his habit, "Now, Reggie, don't make the mistakes I made when I took that biology PhD in '56 and gave up my chances at . . ."

(10 pages later:)

. . . and to make a long story short, that's how I met your Aunt Katharine. And that's how you got here," Uncle Frank concluded. Reggie would have been nonplussed, he had reflected at the time, had he not learned of his mother's illicit affair with Uncle Frank from Cousin Stu months earlier, when Stu had called to tell him about his golf scholarship to Penn, a scholarship which had only rekindled Reggie's bitterness about his mistaken decision to take premed . . .

Here the writer churns out endless scenes establishing background information with no main story in sight. On page 50, the reader still has no idea why it's important to know about Reggie's true parentage, his medical career, or the geography of Montauk. By page 100, the reader would be having strong suspicions that it *isn't* important, were a reader ever to make it as far as page 100.

The writer has also created an entire frame scene in which nothing actually happens. Don't forget that from the reader's perspective, the main story line is what is happening to the protagonist *now*. So whatever Reggie thinks about on the train, the main action is a man sitting and staring out of a window, feeling a little queasy, page after page after page.

Avoid creating scenes merely as places where a character remembers or mulls over background information. The character will have plenty of time to do that in scenes where something actually happens. It would be much more effective, for instance, if Reggie had reservations about his profession in the course of a scene in which he is performing a life-saving operation on his kid brother.

If you find yourself unable to escape a Waiting Room, look honestly at your novel and consider what the first important event is. Everything before that event can probably be cut. If there is important information in that material, how briefly can it be explained? Surprisingly often, twenty pages of text can be replaced by a single paragraph of exposition or interior monologue. If you feel even more drastic measures are called for, see "Radical Surgery for Your Novel," page 11.

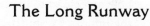

The Long Runway

In which a character's childhood is recounted to no purpose

- 1 -

Reynaldo's first memory was of his mother, the Contessa, dressing for an evening of card playing. That night, the scandalous Marquis vin Diesel came to pick her up in his elegant horse-drawn Louis Quinze brolly. The sight of the matched Angora geldings in the gathering dusk, harnessed in ampersands and cornices after the fashion of the day, would forever be burned into Reynaldo's memory.

"Good night, sweet Prince," his mother called from the door. "Do sleep thou tightly."

"I entreat thee and simper, mother, stay!" baby Reynaldo said, gesturing at the fearful dark behind the damasked street lamps. "Doth there be not danger?"

"Oh, that is a silly Leviathan of thy youthful imaginings," his mother scoffed uproariously, and pulled the door to. She returned later that night unharmed, and gave him a caramel merkin she'd won in a final tempestuous hand of *vingt-fromage*.

- 2 -

Thirty-five years later, Reynaldo tumbled out of bed, laughing heartily at his manservant Hugo, and went about his morning toilette.

Soon, glistening with ambergris and jauntily sprinkling himself with exotic tars and raisins, Reynaldo called out, "No need to tune the pangolin this morning, Hugo, for I have decided to cancel my lesson and rendezvous with the Infanta for shuttlecocks."

For mysterious reasons, many authors consider it useful to provide a story about a forty-year-old man-about-town with a prologue drawn from his life as a five-year-old boy. It is equally common for such authors, in the cause of thoroughness, to go on to provide scenes of the hero at ten, fifteen, and twenty-five before arriving at the age where he will actually do something. Presumably this is meant to yield insights into the hero's character and the key events that formed it, which is a good idea when presenting a paper at a symposium of psychoanalysts. Your reader, however, was hoping for a good yarn. (There's only one letter's difference between "yarn" and "yawn," and it is often a long letter, filled with childhood memories.)

While it is your job to know a great deal about your characters, it is seldom necessary to share it all with the reader, and by "seldom," we mean "never." You, an author, are providing a service to the reader: the service of telling a story. When you call somebody to provide you with a service, the IT guy for example, do you want to hear everything he knows about C++ machine language, SSID encoding, and public key encryption before he tells you how to get back on line?

Radical Surgery for Your Novel
In media res

If your novel is getting bogged down in introductory background information, consider this time-tested kick-start technique.

Pick a pivotal action scene and start your novel in the middle of it, introducing your character when he is already in the midst of some gripping conflict, to get the reader instantly involved. This may be the first exciting event in the novel, but writers sometimes begin with the final climactic confrontation and then use most of the remaining book to bring the reader full circle, back to the big shoot-out, mass suicide, or spaying incident. Once the story has some momentum, you can pause the action to bring the reader up to date with any background information that's necessary.

"Action scene" doesn't mean this technique is limited to novels in which things blow up. "There I was, dressed in nothing but a towel in the most expensive suite in the Plaza Hotel, the man who thought he was marrying a seasonings heiress expected any minute. But that wasn't who I found when I answered the door . . . " works just as well as "There I was, dressed in nothing but a towel in the most expensive suite in the Plaza Hotel, the gunfire from the hallway getting closer and closer . . . "

The Vacation Slide Show

Where the author substitutes location for story

Rah T'uay was much dustier than Bangalot, Chip observed, refastening his backpack. Still he did not know if he would find here the deeper meaning to life that he had come to the East seeking weeks before. Could it be three weeks already? He counted in his head as he sipped the bitter local tea made of tea leaves and piping hot water. One, two, three weeks! It was three!

The first week he had spent among the lush vegetation of Bangalot, where the exotic tendrils of the carnivorous plants were only made more romantic by his chance encounter with Heather, on Spring Break from the U. of M. After their night of romance, it was on by boat to the mountain village of Ruh Ning Tsor, and at last an overnight connection on a bus which always seemed to be on the point of vanishing in the majesty and mysteriousness of the landscape it passed through on the way to the chalky cliffs of the coastal atoll of Suppu Rashon. How he had been forever changed in such a short time!

There was a time when a book could be sold purely because its author had been to distant climes and had returned to tell of the exotic sights he had seen. That author was Marco Polo, and the time was the thirteenth century. If you have particular knowledge of an interesting place, you should certainly use it to give your novel a strong sense of place and its own distinct flavor. But while exotic locales might add a savory tang to your novel, no matter what bazaars you have visited, fascinating con artists you have shared your money with, or ragged street children you have pitied, the criteria for a story in Timbuktu are exactly the same as the criteria in Terre Haute. If Chip does nothing on a tropical island but describe the wonders of being on a tropical island, it is just a Waiting Room with foliage—foliage which, furthermore, the reader has already seen on the Discovery Channel, in HD.

Words Fail Me

Where the author stops short of communication

Now that he had finally reached Paris, Chip understood why they called it the City of Lights. It was the lights! There was something special about Paris that was indescribable. It was so different than being back home in Terre Haute. There was something he couldn't put his finger on, a certain . . . *je ne sais quoi!* He finally understood what they meant by that!

He bit into his Big Mac and, just as he'd always known it would, even a Big Mac tasted different here—the difference was unbelievable! It was something he had entirely missed out on all his life . . . until now. It was awesome.

Ah, Paris! City of Lights!

A subcategory of the Vacation Slide Show consists of those novels in which the value of the exotic location exists only in the author's remembered experience of it, which experience burns so brightly in the author's mind that he does not realize he has failed to convey in any concrete way the physical, or even emotional, reality of the location to the reader. Unlike the Vacation Slide Show, there was *never* a time when this kind of novel could be sold, because it does not even let the reader see the sights. It is the equivalent of showing slides of your visit to Machu Picchu, in which you stand in the foreground of each shot, smiling and gesturing at Machu Picchu but also blocking Machu Picchu from view. Your reader is not sharing your experience. Your reader is thinking, "What the hell is that behind him? It looks like it might be Machu Picchu. Or maybe a McDonald's."

This technique is not limited to descriptions of exotic places; words like "amazing" and "unbelievable" can be used to obscure any experience, event, or setting (see Part III, "Style—The Basics," for further discussion).

The Gum on the Mantelpiece

In which the reader is unintentionally misled

Irina entered the nursery to ensure a fire would be roaring when her two beloved sisters arrived. Before bending to stir the coals, she plucked from her mouth the moist pink wad of gum she had been chewing since coming to Petersburg from the family's country estate. The mantelpiece was bare, and Irina planted the large, wet bolus of gum firmly upon it.

At that precise instant, Uncle Vanya, passing through the conservatory, paused at the piano to play one eerie, dissonant chord, which seemed to hang suspended in the air, presaging misfortunes to come.

"Irina!" Masha said with delight, entering the nursery. Her cheeks were pink from the wintry winds, and cold still rose up off her thick and luxurious furs. Of the three, Masha had always been the most fashionable, and treasured her furs more than anything, except perhaps for her beloved sisters. Masha threw her arms wide and crossed the room to embrace dear Irina, the sleeve of her most beloved sable coming very very close to the sticky lump of gum, kept soft and warm and really sticky by the flames that now leapt below it as it lurked there on the mantelpiece, nearly itself a glowering presence in the room, hungry and malevolent, like a sea anemone waiting for prey to swim by. It seemed only through some divine intervention that the sleeve was unharmed.

"Irina! Masha!" cried Natasha, as she entered the room to see them warmly embracing. Natasha was the prettiest, and the most vain, and her sisters had lovingly teased her since they were little about her long blonde hair, which she wore always loose, though it wasn't the custom.

Just as Natasha ran to her sisters, an ominous wind blew through an open window and lifted up her long, beautiful hair to swirl about her shoulders, floating like a defenseless blonde cloud, innocent and unaware of any danger, only *millimetres*—counted in the French style— from the gum on the mantelpiece.

"Come, let us go to another room and slowly reveal to each other our unhappinesses!" Natasha said.

"Yes! Let's do!" said Masha, and the three departed.

*   *   *

Later that day, Uncle Vanya came in from the cherry orchard and cleaned up the gum.

The good news is that as a writer of fiction you get to create your world from scratch. The bad news is that because you create your world from scratch, everything in it is a conscious choice, and the reader will assume that there is some reason behind these choices. Sloppiness in these matters can lead to any number of unintended consequences, foremost among them what is known by writers as the Gum on the Mantelpiece. This is an element introduced in the beginning of a novel that seems so significant that the reader can't help but keep one eye on it, wondering when it will come into play. If it does not, your reader will feel unfairly dealt with. Remember: *if there is gum on the mantelpiece in the first chapter, it must go on something by the last chapter.*

For similar reasons, details that would go unremarked in real life—a quick glance across the room, the lyrics of the song that's playing when you enter a bar— take on much greater significance in fiction. If *you* have to run dripping from the shower to sign for an unexpected package, it is probably the gardening clogs you forgot you ordered from Lands' End. But if your character is interrupted in the shower by the arrival of an unexpected package, it tells your readers that the package will unleash a momentous chain of events.

Two particularly common versions follow.

Oh, Don't Mind Him

Where a character's problems remain unexplored

The river had never looked so beautiful and wild as it did that Friday morning in April. Fed by the melting snows of the mountains that towered grandly to our west, the icy clear waters rushed by around our waders, my brother's and mine, as we watched the rainbow flash of the trout in a companionable silence.

My brother, just back from the War, seemed restless, and though I was only a boy of eighteen, I recognized the smell of rum that hung about him like the clouds of midges that would descend on us those afternoons. And I saw my brother's anger flare when our somber meditations were broken by the loud, coarse laughter of two sportsmen up from Michigan, making their clumsy way through our woods. He seemed to feel my concern, and smiled through the sweat that glistered over his reddened face.

"War can do things to a man, Chip," he confessed, and then for the first time openly took out his flask. "When the black hound gets down into your soul, it will set its teeth into all your youthful dreamings."

I wanted to quiz him about this black hound, but forgot to ask and never had reason to think of it again, for the next day, uncomfortably dressed in my grandfather's suit, I was seated in a Pullman car of the Union Pacific, off to begin my great adventure at Yale.

In real life, people are riddled with chronic problems that are not addressed for long periods of time, if ever. But in fiction, all problems are just the opening chords of a song. If there is a brother who has a problem with alcohol, a child who has lost her dog, or even someone whose car has simply broken down, the reader will worry about those people and expect the author to do something about it. All such problems need their own little plot arc to give the reader closure. But subplots can easily start to spread and take over your novel. Often you would do better to focus your reader's empathy on the problems of your main character.

The Deafening Hug

The unintended love interest

Anna put her arms around her brother and held him close. He could smell her faint perfume, and the warmth of her body made all his troubles drain away. She had filled out since going away to college, and the gentle, persistent, pressure of her breasts was distinct through her thin T-shirt. He let her go at last and said, with a slight blush, "Why can't I talk to Amanda the way I talk to you?"

Anna laughed, but couldn't meet his eyes. "I don't know. Maybe 'cause she's beautiful?"

Hal choked on his response. To him, no one could ever be as beautiful as his little sister. If only she could see herself as others saw her! But he drove these ideas from his head. He had to concentrate on his troubles with Amanda, even if he was beginning to suspect he would have to look elsewhere for the real passion he was determined to find.

Sometimes the author is the last to know. It is all too easy to create a love interest where none is wanted. We call this the Deafening Hug for obvious reasons, and for reasons just as obvious, it should be avoided. Versions include:

- *The Mayfly Fatale.* A new character is described as "a handsome, muscular man with raven hair and a cheeky grin" or "a lissome blonde bombshell in a tight tank top." The reader immediately thinks this is a love/sex interest. While real life is full of attractive people who—let's face it—never look at you twice, protagonists live in a charmed world where it is assumed that all the attractive people they notice are already halfway to the boudoir.

- *Alice in Lapland.* Any undue interest in or physical contact with children will set off alarms. If you do not want your reader to think he is reading about a pedophile, dandling of children on knees should be kept to a minimum by fathers, and even more so by uncles. If your character is in any way associated with organized religion, whether he is a bishop, a minister, or the kindly old church caretaker with a twinkle in his eye, he should not even pull a child from a burning building.

- *We're Going to Need a Bigger Closet.* Male friends hug, toast their friendship, and later stumble drunkenly to sleep in the cabin's one bed. The reader is way ahead of you—they are secretly gay, and nothing you say later is going to change his mind. If you do not intend them to be secretly gay, let Alan sleep on the couch.

The Red Herring on the Mantelpiece

A red herring is a well-planted false clue, sleight of hand that makes the reader watch one thing while you are busy doing another thing, a thing that will surprise and delight the reader when it is revealed at a time of your choosing.

The *inadvertently* misleading element, "The Gum on

the Mantelpiece," can sometimes be turned into a red herring and made to work for you instead of against you. If your novel is feeling a bit thin because too little is going on (see "Monogamy," page 21), the addition of a decent red herring can lend it some substance and depth. By tying things together and creating a greater sense of interrelatedness, you can convert mantelpiece gum into incarnadine fish.

A classic red herring is the obvious suspect in a whodunit (the smirking gigolo with a hair-trigger temper, the perverse countess) who looks increasingly suspect—until the last scene, when the culprit turns out to be someone else entirely. An equally time-honored herring is the shallow Lothario the heroine is in love with for 200 pages, or so she thinks.

Always make sure your red herring is an integral part of the story. When you perform sleight of hand, every movement should seem natural. So the murder suspect should be a character who is an established part of the world of the novel—typically it's the lover, close relative, or long-time colleague of the detective or the cadaver. We will not feel the same pleasure in being misled if the suspect is just an unlucky stranger who trips over the still-warm corpse in the dark and, in falling, catches hold of the murder weapon, leaving a perfect set of fingerprints.

And when your red herring no longer serves a purpose, do not simply drop it, leaving a frustratingly loose thread. When the lover is rejected, we want to see his reaction. The heroine will also be thinking about his feelings, and a failure to address these points will erode the reader's sense that the character is real.

2

COMPLICATIONS AND PACING

Twenty-two minutes later, he realized it was like time had stopped.

So your novel has a rock-solid setup, and it's heading toward an amazing, explosive conclusion. Never fear! There's still plenty of time to squash excitement like a bug. Read on for the fascinating lore of "bogging down in the middle."

Plot Basics: Thread Count

There is a sweet spot for every novel—the right number of characters, the right number of events—where your plot achieves a realistic complexity without requiring color-coded pages to follow it. We cannot tell you what yours is, but we can tell you what it probably is not.

Monogamy
Here there is only one plot line, and the only thing your

characters do is follow it. If, by page 50, you have only two characters playing a role in the plot—Chapter One, they meet; Chapter Two, the first date; Chapter Three, first kiss—your novel is probably suffering from a bad case of monogamy. Even if it is a light-hearted romance set in the bistros and boutiques of Manhattan, there's something *Twilight Zone*–ish about it. The only real people in it are your two main characters, who do not interact in any significant way with anybody but each other.

There are many problems with this. Some of them—tedium, boredom, monotony—are merely symptomatic. But one in particular makes it fatal. It does not feel like real life. However obsessed Annabel is with dating Ronald, she still has to go to work, deal with her family, score the painkillers to which she has been addicted since high school. In a monogamy plot, friends and relatives only ever call the protagonist in order to have long conversations about Ronald's behavior on dinner dates. In real life, friends and relatives only call to have long conversations about themselves.

Onanism

In its most extreme form, monogamy is better termed onanism. Here a single character goes through life without having any meaningful interaction with anyone else in the world. If a typical page of your novel features only one character, you are probably engaged in onanism. Into this category go all stories about sad singles who spend scene after scene thinking about the mess in their apartment, their flabby body, the distorted faces of the hostile strangers who surround them, their unhappy childhood, the last job they lost, and their habit of onanism. Tales of solo travel and/or self-discovery are particularly susceptible.

Serial Monogamy

Some authors cannot bear suspense. As soon as the protagonist has a problem, the author rushes in officiously to solve it. If Joe Protagonist loses his job, his sister phones him as he is leaving the office to offer him a much better job, or he is happily reminded of a job offer he had previously neglected. Fighting spouses make up immediately; ailments speedily respond to medication; lost keys are found in the first place Joe looks—*phew*! These novels seem to be based on a to-do list of plot complications, resulting in plots such as:

1. Find Joe new job
2. Find Joe new girlfriend
3. Fall of Communism
4. Find Joe new socks
5. Epiphany

If a problem is worth creating, it's worth hanging on to long enough to make the reader care. Most are worth hanging on to until the very end, when all loose ends are cunningly tied together in a rousing climax.

The Orgy

Here, innumerable plot lines confound the reader. Chapter One introduces a Nazi living in hiding and the Jewish private investigator with whom he plays chess; Chapter Two introduces an ordinary housewife whose husband is cheating on her with the Nazi, now revealed to be gay; Chapter Three is from the point of view of a homeless child living in Haiti who will not meet the other characters until page 241; in Chapter Four we learn about a murder cover-up in the Vatican through a flashback to the house-wife's childhood . . .

And by the Way, I'm an Expert Marksman

Where the pay-off is not set up

As the water crept up higher and higher, Jack realized the hydraulics had failed, and he would have to swim under water the length of the now-submerged hallway if he was to save Synthya. The situation looked hopeless. Fortunately, the years Jack had spent among the pearl divers of the South Pacific following a shipwreck had trained him to hold his breath for nearly fourteen minutes, surpassing the ability of most Westerners.

If your hero is going to save the day through some very special-ized skill late in the book, it is best to introduce that skill early on and make it a part of your character's life. Jack might swim regu-larly for exercise, or pick up walking-around money through bar bets. He could stay in touch with his adoptive mother and father in Polynesia. In all these cases, he could recall and even showcase this uncanny breath-holding ability. When the submerged hallway appears, the reader has the satisfaction of seeing disparate elements coming together.

No matter how you do it, it cannot come as a complete surprise when it is revealed to the reader in the second to last chapter that Earl the lumberjack was once the ballroom dance champion of the Upper Peninsula, a skill which allows him to charm the snooty Lubricia, when dancing had not been previously mentioned. (For further discussion, see "Why Your Job Is Harder Than God's," page 28.)

Rose-Colored Half-Full Glasses

Where the setup reveals the pay-off

Jack surveyed the rising water with a smile. With his almost instinctive understanding of hydraulics, he knew it would only take five minutes to swim down that corridor under water, something he could easily achieve with his skills. It was good to know Synthya wasn't in any real danger.

He filled his lungs as he had learned to do, and plunged into the water, easily swimming the length of the hall and coming up out of the water at the other end scarcely out of breath. There stood Synthya, wreathed in smiles. It had been exactly as he'd suspected: nothing to be concerned about at all. He even had the keys, so getting out of here would be no problem.

"But we still have to escape from this locked room," Synthya said, her face subsiding into a frown.

He pulled the keys out of his pocket with a smile.

"Oh, great," she said, and they went to the door, unlocking it easily and walking out to safety.

We wouldn't want to create any anxiety in the reader, now, would we? That might lead to suspense, which might lead to a book sale—and, God forbid, royalties.

Do not reassure your reader that everything is going to turn out all right. Sometimes even a sense of confidence in the hero can amount to a tip-off that the happy ending is a foregone conclusion. The hero is better off considering the odds to be almost impossible—but resolving to try, even if it means losing his life. A related problem is:

Déjà Vu

Where the setup deflates the pay-off

The past eight hours had been the greatest martyrdom Jack had ever endured. He was barely able to lift the crippled Synthya to rescue her from the now deadly office. As Jack carried her out to safety, groaning at the strain on his already injured back, suddenly Doctor Nefaro, the renegade ergonomics expert, stood in front of them, wielding his army-issue .68 Grump automatic pistol.

Don't panic, Jack told himself. *All you need to do is get in a blow to his wrist. That will make him drop the gun, and you can duck, slipping Synthya to the ground unharmed, and knock him out with the butt.*

"Going somewhere?" sneered Nefaro. He leered at Synthya, lecherously and salaciously.

"Yeah, we're going home, and then we're going to get married," said Jack breezily.

"I don't know how you're going to do that—when you're *dead*!"

Jack sprang into action. Dealing Doctor Nefaro a blow on the wrist, he made him drop the gun. Jack then ducked, slipping Synthya to the ground unharmed, grabbed the gun, and clubbed Nefaro on the head, dropping him to his knees. Soon Nefaro was stretched out unconscious on the ground.

"That will teach you to design chairs that place undue pressure on the lower lumbar structure!" Jack cried in victory.

It is always a good idea to avoid letting the reader know what is going to happen before it happens. If a character details a plan of action before executing it, blunders or unforeseen circumstances should always arise, causing the plan to go awry. For instance, Nefaro could reveal that he has hidden a bomb with the playground equipment just now being shipped, and only he knows the code that will disarm it. Or the blow to the wrist could trigger a subcutaneous device that activates Synthya's programming. Or Nefaro could be killed outright, followed by Jack's stunned realization that Nefaro had been talking to somebody standing behind him—none other than the true criminal mastermind behind the carpal tunnel–inducing keyboards.

When there is a plan, things cannot go according to it. If they do, the plan becomes a spoiler, the action becomes dull and predictable, and the reader's plan to finish your book is what gets derailed.

Why Your Job Is Harder Than God's

"But that really happened to my friend!"

In real life, no matter how unlikely anything is—the deaths of William Shakespeare and Miguel de Cervantes on the same date in 1616, or one man being struck by lightning five times—if it really happens, we do not question that it *would* happen. Our credulity is not stretched to the breaking point, causing us to stop participating in the world and go looking for another one that is more convincing. Thus, God can work with the most mind-bending coincidences, far-fetched plot devices, and perverse dramatic ironies, never giving a moment's thought to whether or not his audience will buy it. You do not have that luxury.

When a writer proposes an unlikely event, we buy it or not based on whether the writer has managed to create a world in which the event is interrelated with everything around it, so it appears to the reader something that might naturally happen. Unlikely strokes of good fortune do not appear from nowhere; we arrive at the discovery of the briefcase of cash with some inkling of the chain of events that led to it being in the hotel closet. What might appear to the characters as amazing good luck should for the reader have a certain feeling of inevitability. We are made to understand that a character behaved in a particular way because of the person she is; she does not suddenly break character to do the one thing that is most convenient for the author.

Strokes of good luck and mind-boggling coincidences can be used *when that is what your novel is about*. A character whose problems are miraculously resolved when he finds a duffel bag filled with unmarked currency will be received by the reader very differently than a character whose problems *begin* when he finds the money.

So, in a good novel, the writer strives for a balance of likelihood and contingency: the more unlikely an event, the more deeply rooted and widely integrated it should be into the chapters that came before it. Above all, the writer does not assume that an event in his novel is believable simply because "it really happened to this guy I know!"

Zeno's Manuscript

In which irrelevant detail derails narrative momentum

"Just wait here, you stud. I'm going to change into something more comfortable," Lubricia promised. She went into the bathroom and locked the door. Then she took off her sensible shoes, setting them side by side near the bathtub. Next to go were her jeans, which stuck a little over her hips, causing her to curse under her breath. Here she paused to inspect her makeup in the mirror. There was a little smudge of mascara under her eyes, which she wiped away with a wetted tissue. She went to the hamper and began to hunt for the sexy negligee she'd left there the day before. She pulled out a sweater, two pairs of pants, several odd socks . . .

Any scene can be killed by description of every meaningless component of whatever action the character undertakes. As in Zeno's Paradox, in which an arrow never reaches its target because it must always travel half the remaining distance, the reader begins to feel as if the end is further and further away.

Special versions include:

On My Way to the Scene

A common (near-epidemic) version is the transport scene, in which characters are shown traveling to the place where something of interest finally occurs. The result is often similar to what happens when somebody pocket-dials your voice mail while out doing errands.

The Bedridden Scene

Any scene in which a character is shown waking up in bed or getting into bed is deeply suspect, unless there is someone *new* in bed with her.

The Plot Not Taken

In which irrelevant options derail narrative momentum

It might have seemed more natural for him to have waited for Lubricia to come out of the bathroom, and had his way with her. At least he could have explained why he was leaving. It would have been possible for him to leave a note, even. But his intimacy issues and his inability to sit through long descriptions of meaningless actions, had made him leave without saying goodbye. He could still call her from this phone booth he was passing. No, that one looked too dirty. Maybe a different phone booth, this one coming up? Really, though, he hated using them at all; they just ate your change and the call never went through. Besides, he had his cell phone with him.

Should he call? What if she was still in the bathroom, brushing each tooth individually? No, better that he . . .

Sometimes an author gets bogged down in explaining the reasons that the character *didn't* do all the things he could have done. This approach has clear risks, as all possible human actions might eventually be represented, requiring a novel of several million pages just to get Joe out of bed in the morning. It is generally best to apply the pruning shears and concentrate on what the character is in fact doing.

The Benign Tumor

Where an apparently meaningful development isn't

Candida couldn't help but think that her condition was a mixed blessing. After the diagnosis, her boyfriend had shown his true colors, for one thing.

And, of course, she would never have met Dr. Albicans. The question that faced her now was whether to let him perform the risky experimental procedure that he wanted to do. She reached into her bag for a cigarette, and instead she found the pamphlet that sweet young girl had handed her in the waiting room. NATURAL HEALING FOR YOUR CONDITION.

Maybe it was time to take this a little more seriously.

Candida went to her desk and fired up the computer, and was soon exploring a whole new world.

(There follow fifty pages in which Candida considers unconventional treatments and meets a number of people who practice alternative medicine and recommend it to her, one after another.)

> Back home, she looked at the pamphlet on the counter one more time before dropping it into the trash. "No," she said, shaking her head wistfully; "natural healing just isn't for me."

The Benign Tumor is a scene, chapter, or entire section of a novel that can be neatly excised without any harm to the surrounding organism. While the world of alternative medicine is, like many other things, potentially interesting to explore in a novel, it is ultimately frustrating to the reader when it is deployed in a way that leaves both the protagonist and the story unchanged. First drafts are the natural habitat of such scenes; handily, revisions are hunting season, and there is no limit to how many you can bag.

And before you object—no, they are not worth saving even if they have "my most beautiful writing" in them. Such passages are like baby pictures: endlessly fascinating to the parent, of passing interest to friends and relatives, and of no interest to anyone else at all.

Mr. Sandman, on Second Thought, Bring Me a Gun

_____ *Wherein characters dream*

> That night, Ralph had the strangest dream he had had in years. He and his wife Missy were in a court which was

being presided over by Leonard Cohen. Ralph looked around, and all the jury members were also Leonard Cohen.

"How do you plead?" Judge Cohen said, sneering at Ralph.

"I plead not squid," Ralph replied—which at the time seemed perfectly sensible to him.

At this, all the Leonard Cohens grew long tentacles and began to converge on Missy. They wrapped their tentacles around her, but she seemed rather to enjoy than dislike the contact.

Finally, Ralph cried "Ink! Ink!" and found that he had the power to squirt a paralyzing ink out of his eyes. But he could only do it if he believed in himself, and Missy's indifference to her ravishment made him freeze. He tried to move forward, but it was as if his feet each weighed two thousand pounds . . . at this point, the scene changed to colonial Latin America. The Leonard Cohens were gone, and he was with a gypsy woman who looked nothing like Missy, but Ralph knew inside himself that it was Missy . . . And he knew that marrying her had been a mistake. Nothing much happened in the rest of that dream, but he had another one later in the night, in which . . .

Early twentieth-century fiction was newly awash in Freudianism, and no respectable novelist would send his book out into the world without a layer of symbolism, dramatizing the unconscious fears and desires of his characters. This was often accomplished by presenting the character's dreams, usually in a font called Stream-of-Consciousness Italic.

Science rushes onward, and it is now understood that reading page after page of characters' dreams about building walls with bricks of anguish is about as interesting as, well, listening to an actual stranger tell you about his actual dreams.

A good approach is to allow one dream per novel. Then, in the final revision, go back and get rid of that, too.

The Second Argument in the Laundromat

A scene which occurs twice

"I can't believe that only two weeks after our wedding you would do this!" Synthya cried. "You had such a promising future with your family's hydraulics firm, and you quit to work in ergonomics without even discussing it with me?"

"It's my life, not yours! My career!" Jack said, his anger getting the best of him.

Synthya began to cry. "What happened to everything you promised me, that we'd share everything, that we were partners? You're out every night now at parties associated with that new ergonomics crowd, and I'm left here in the laundromat washing your clothes! It's as if you were ashamed of me and didn't respect my opinion."

"I told you we'd get a washer/dryer after I'd paid off the student loans."

"That's what you think the problem is, Jack? That's what you have to say for yourself?" Synthya said, turning away from him.

(Ten pages later, after an intervening scene of office politics at Jack's new job, and another night out drinking with his fellow ergonomicists:)

"Hey, baby! Those guys are crazy! Wait'll you hear the latest," Jack said, coming into the laundromat late.

Synthya ignored him and continued folding laundry.

"Oh," Jack sighed. "What is it now?"

"Nothing. But you could have let me know you'd be at work late, or maybe even invited me to join you and that cool new crowd of yours."

"This is about buying the washer/dryer again, isn't it? You know why I'm short of money right now."

"Oh, Jack," Synthya said, and started crying.

NEVER use two scenes to establish the same thing. We do not, under any circumstances, want a series of scenes in which the hero goes to job interviews but fails to get the job, or has a series of unsuccessful dates to illustrate bad luck in love. This works in the movies, where three scenes can pass in thirty seconds, but not in a novel. Unless a new character or plot element is introduced, once is enough. Related problems:

Last Night, When We Had
the Argument in the Laundromat

Characters have a long talk describing to each other all the things they have done in the last scene. Even if that scene had them killing Godzilla just before he destroyed the nuclear power plant, this is not a new scene at all but the same scene again, by other means.

Let's Go to the Laundromat to Talk About This

Characters begin talking at home, then go to the laundromat and continue the same conversation. Even when the substance of what's said in the laundromat includes new information, this reads as two scenes that are essentially the same.

Oh, and Also?

In which too much reminiscing stalls the story

Joe saw Anne waiting on the corner, and immediately remembered the first time they'd met. She was eighteen then, just out of high school, walking her poodle in the wrong part of town. He was the gentleman who gave her a ride.

Now she saw him and waved. He pulled over to the curb. She was wearing the same green cotton dress she'd worn when they went to the Caribbean. He would never forget that trip. The weather was perfect the first few days. Then the skies opened; but they'd amused them-selves well enough!

"Hi, Anne," he said, as she got into his Ford Fromage. "How was your day?"

"I don't know," she shrugged, grinning. That was so like her. It was also like her mother, Joe remembered. He had known Anne's mother before he'd ever met Anne. In 1963, when he was only eight . . .

Here everything reminds the point-of-view character of something else. It's like trying to leave the house with someone who keeps realizing they've left something inside. Then something else. Then something else. With this constant application of the brakes, the plot has no chance of ever getting where it's going.

The Padded Cell

The late twentieth century forever changed the lives of writers in two important ways. The first was the fall of Communism, which threatened to deprive the thriller-writing community, along with the military-industrial complex, of its *raison d'etre*. Fortunately, writers of thrillers, like the Pentagon, soon discovered or invented new bad guys.

The second was not so easily dealt with. With the introduction of the cell phone, dozens of situations writers had relied on since they were banging out stories for the pulps at a penny a word were suddenly rendered moot.

In a stand-off with a killer in a warehouse in a deserted part of Brooklyn? Duh! 911!

Monster got you cornered in a shack in Appalachia? Well, what network are you with?

The horrible truth is that even if the crisis comes in the Tibetan Himalayas, the contemporary reader will tend to think "What, they don't get reception there?" and the contemporary reader will have a point.

The primitive methods that writers conjured to fight back in the early and mid-nineties had cell phones forgotten and batteries running down right and left, but as time went on the readers, writers, and phones all became more sophisticated. Below, some gambits by category.

Forgetting of Phone
In the credibility arms race, this is the pointy stick. However, pointy sticks are not without their uses, and forgetting is

sometimes plausible—fire or flood wakes character, who rushes half asleep from bed at 4 a.m., say. In such cases, overexplaining with a more sophisticated gambit could be less credible. The key is to show the character rushing precipitously from the house long before the character needs the phone.

Loss of Phone

Was your character dangling upside down from a helicopter at any point? If the closest your character comes to this scenario is traveling to work on the crosstown bus, readers might balk.

Destruction of Phone, by Villain

Because this act clearly springs from the villain's motivations, this is quite workable and is similar to the time-honored "Jim! They've cut the phone lines!" Note, however, that phone lines were never actually in the hero's pants pocket at the time of the cutting, so the cell phone version demands more finesse.

Swallowing of Phone, by Shark

Where the shark is your character's antagonist, it might be finessed. Where the shark is randomly passing through the scene, note how close this is to "The shark ate my homework." This holds true for any bear, zombie, or Dread Cthulhu who might similarly have a taste for electronics.

Failure of Signal or Battery

The more baldly convenient to the author, the less chance of success.

Usurpation of Technology by Demonic Possession, Teenage Hackers, or HAL-like Intelligence

Great where genre appropriate; not otherwise recommended.

Quirk of Character

A character might indeed refuse to own a cell phone because he subscribes to outré theories about cancer risks or wiretapping, but this works best when he is engaged in an enterprise (exposing radiation cover-ups, drug dealing) that lends itself to such theories. Do not have your hero, a Hollywood agent, announce airily that she can't stand the things.

Setting of Novel in Past

Ideal. When action is early twentieth century, however, caution dictates that the character should make a call on a period phone early in the novel (*"Operator! Get me Butterfield 8!" he said, his head dwarfed by the primitive mechanism*) to drive the point home to younger readers, who may be under the vague impression that cell phones were invented by Galileo.

3

ENDINGS

And Jesus lived happily ever after.

What if, despite your best efforts, your story begins with an exciting premise and gathers momentum through purposeful and surprising scenes? Don't worry—it's still possible to drive away editors by writing an implausible, irrelevant ending. Here are some of our favorites.

But a Meteor *Could* Land There, Right?

In which the author cheats

It had all come down to this.

Thirteen short weeks ago, Rafael had been just another Adjunct Professor of Symbolology hoping for nothing more than to publish enough papers on his specialty, symbologolonics, to get on a tenure track and start thinking about retirement.

Then he had met Fafnir, the beautiful and exotic

stranger who claimed to have proof of a secret society that had guarded a symbolologicolonical secret for two millennia. The secret had taken them breathlessly across three continents, and they had been tested by many life-threatening situations, while each had discovered new facets of him- or herself, and also fell in love, though they had not yet "done it."

But now, here they were, cornered at the edge of a cliff with no possible route of escape from the deadly oncoming Thing from which they could not possibly escape, though they still had a few last moments to discuss the hopelessness of their situation and kiss each other goodbye.

Suddenly, they heard the "thwack-thwack-thwack" sound of a helicopter overhead.

"Look," said Fafnir, pointing up.

They scrambled up the rope ladder that was lowered to them, narrowly escaping the Thing that was menacing them so menacingly. Once they were in the passenger cabin, they stared with surprise at the wealthy industrialist, who appraised them with a quirked brow.

"So you're the pair who have been causing all the trouble, eh?"

"Who are you?" Rafael asked, awed by his fancy clothes.

"I am Barrington Hewcott, richest man in the world, and I have decided that this has gone on for long enough. Now you two just sit back, and I'll have you home in a jiff."

Endings are the last refuge of the implausible, or so it would seem from all the climactic moments that come from so far beyond left field that they make left field look like right field.

The reader is invested in seeing the hero resolve his problems himself, and feels disappointed when he doesn't. Further, by introducing a previously unmentioned element to resolve a situation, the author is suddenly changing the rules of his fictional world. This is as much fun as when somebody suddenly and unilaterally changes the rules of a game you are playing. It is as if the author had said, "Oh, I just realized my plot doesn't work, so I'm going to add something from outside of my plot, okay?"

Okay! And we're going to add something to the recycling.

This particular blunder is known as *deus ex machina*, which is French for "Are you fucking kidding me?"

"And One Ring to Bind Them!" Said the Old Cowpoke

Where the author switches genres in midstream

Last day of summer

2 ciggies, 3 Cosmos, 1750 nonalcohol calories

Dear Diary:
Well, this summer has been one headlong dive into whirlwind romance for me. Ha! I wish! As you know, I've spent most of the summer trying to run into Percy Marlborough (sigh!), the handsome young industrialist I met the day I snuck into the country club on a lark. You know, diary, when Billy, my best friend since college days, who is unhappily married but loves animals and children, dared me to?

If you were to go back and read yourself, diary, you'd see three hundred pages—I'm such a silly chatterbox—

of me mooning over Percy, worrying about my weight, going to work at my semi-glamorous job at a publication, shopping, shopping, shopping, and then coming home to eat Ben & Jerry's while watching TV—and talking *back* to it!

Well, I should go. Billy's coming over. He says he has something important to tell me.

The next day

Dear Diary:
You'll never believe it! Billy's wife somehow died! And he says he loves me! I think I see him completely differently now!

I'll have to keep this short, because Billy rented a cute little cottage in the country and we're going to spend a weekend together. This could lead to anything! I bought some sexy new underwear, just in case. Giggle.

One week later

OH GOD OH GOD OH GOD. He's not human.

If anyone finds this, I beg you, call the police. Tell them our city is full of insect-lizard creatures that walk invisibly among us and feed on our emotions, an ancient, eldritch race that see all our efforts and strivings as no more than the caperings of monkeys. I am writing this in my own blood, as it runs from my fingertips, pulpy and raw from clawing at the unfinished walls of this dank basement. Tell the police, tell the newspapers, and then run. It's too late for me, but

OH GOD OH GOD OH GOD I think he's coming back. OH GOD OH GOD OH GOD . . .

Old rules have been thrown to the wind, and genres are now mixed with wild abandon. Paranormal romance. Noir science fiction. Vampires on Wall Street. Love among the runes. It's fresh and fertile ground, and we encourage it. However, if you are going to bring in an otherworldly, fantastic, or science-fictional element, it's a very good idea not to wait until the last twenty pages.

While a revelatory moment at the end of a novel that causes the reader to think back and understand everything in a whole new light—oh, it was the *uncle* telling the story the whole time!—is a fine thing, you may NOT inform the reader after three hundred pages of quotidian realism that the scrappy puppy the hero saved from the fire in Chapter Two is really a magic, mind-reading puppy from another planet, who has just been waiting for the right moment to reveal his superpowers and save the day.

This type of ending is a special instance of *deus ex machina*, known as the *folie adieu*, which is French for "Are you *FUCKING* kidding me?"

Surprise endings must take place in a world in which that surprise can occur. You don't have to march a ghost through Chapter Three to reveal a ghost in Chapter Twelve, but there should have previously been some ghostly happenings, some discussion of ghosts, or an atmosphere that is consistent with the possibility of ghosts.

The Underpants Gnomes

Where crucial steps are omitted

Synthya stared him down unforgivingly. "No, Jack. There's no room for your ergo-draulic ideas in America— or in my heart!"

With that, she slammed the door behind her. In a single day, Jack had lost everything: his struggle against the dangerous ideas of Nefaro, his fight for his father's approval, and finally his bride! He knew there must be a way to make things right—but how???

CHAPTER TWENTY-FIVE

Jack could hardly believe he was back—back in the Executive Room of Bilge Hydraulics. He looked across the table at his beautiful wife, Synthya, whose air of contentment was unmistakable.

"A toast!" said Jack's father, Steve "Pumper" Bilge, proudly sporting the Bilge family crest, which in males generally developed in adolescence.

"Hear hear!" said Professor Nefaro, Jack's ergonomics thesis instructor.

Jack humbly raised his glass of fluid.

"For years, I have struggled to reconcile my patrimony in hydraulics with the call of ergonomics, and to make Synthya and my father understand why I must do what I do. I almost can't believe that everything has somehow worked out so well."

They all stopped to reflect upon the complicated chain of circumstances that had gotten them from there to here.

"But it has, Jack!" Synthya said, raising her fluid to him. "Thanks to you!"

In an early episode of *South Park*, missing underpants led to the discovery of the Underpants Gnomes, who revealed to the boys their not completely thought-out business plan.

1. Collect underpants
2. ???
3. Profit!

Sometimes a writer knows where she wants to end up but can see no plausible way to get from A to Q. Instead, she announces "Q!" in a confident tone, often following up with some vague comments about "long conversations had led to this," or "fevered negotiations had been required, and somehow all issues were finally resolved," or, worst of all, "It was as if John had somehow turned into a different man." If John somehow turns into a different man and we do not witness that transformation, the editor considering your novel will somehow turn into an editor considering a different novel.

The good news is that you still have three quarters of a novel. Go back and write forward from the moment you dropped the ball, allowing that you might end up somewhere other than you had planned.

Goodbye, Cruel Reader!

Where an inconvenient character
is conveniently disposed of

Nefaro realized now that it was never to be. He had worked, he had slaved, he had clawed his way to the position of Vice President of Fluid Transport, Uphill. It had not been without its rewards. He had loved the power, the glamour, the luxuries—luxuries he could no longer do without. But the whole time he'd had his eyes on a bigger prize—Vice President of Fluid Transport, Downhill. Yes, that was his goal; only then would he be able to put his feet up and coast. But no, only Jack Bilge, of Bilge Hydraulics, would ever sit in that chair. And now Nefaro was the only thing that stood in the way of the big merger. He was nothing but an obstruction; he felt like a fly in somebody else's ointment. Nefaro's hand shook as he cocked the .68 Grump and pressed the muzzle to his temple. For a moment hope flared in him—was there a way out? No! It had all gone too far. Damn that merger! As he pulled the trigger he hoped there would be a way to atone for all his sins in the other world.

The primary sin here is lousy plotting. Seeing no way of getting the protagonist out of a thorny plot problem she has created, the author decides to kill whomever stands in his way. She is essentially doing the wetwork for the hero, so he can walk away squeaky clean. This, however, is suicide not only for the villain but for the book deal.

This approach is equally unwelcome if the suicide (freak accident, etc.) befalls the inconvenient wife, the professional rival, or any other character whose absence would be suspiciously convenient to the author. The reader instantly smells foul play. If a character must handily perish, at least lay the groundwork (suicidal ideation, heart condition) in previous scenes.

The lesser version of this, involving sudden transfers to the Tokyo office and the like, also requires preparation.

The Manchurian Parallax of the Thetan Conspiracy Enigma

In which backstory overwhelms story

"You see, the hotel lobbies were all in bed with the Commissioner," Herr Schlock explained, keeping the barrel of the .69 Crosspatch trained on Mary's face. "Whose real name is Joseph Mengele—ring a bell? He escaped to Paraguay after the fall of Berlin, got radical plastic surgery, and began life again as Josephine Womengele. She/he had a brief career as a courtesan in the highest echelons of Washington society that more than prepared him/her to seduce your silly boyfriend, Bruce. It was all part of a long-forgotten fail-safe plan to assassinate President Dukakis, should he have gotten elected. When Bruce inadvertently used that specific combination of coins in the laundromat, it activated the plan and brought him to the attention of Mengele, and so Bruce ended up in bed with the Commissioner, too, in his own way."

Schlock laughed in his German accent as Mary struggled to add up all this new information. Schlock added, "Of course, this may be hard for you to digest after the operation removing your memories that our Canadian enemies put you through, but which was only partly successful—but I can explain all that in the submarine on our way to bomb Winnipeg."

"But that's crazy!" Mary protested. "Up until now the only clue we've had was a frozen leg of mutton!"

Some books end with a long explanation of the mysteries in the plot that is more complex and elaborate than the novel that led to it. This problem is most common in thrillers, but even in romance novels, the hero's cold behavior is sometimes accounted for by a summarized subplot that spans four generations and three wars.

Please make the surprising explanation for a mystery simple enough that it does not substitute pure confusion for amazement. Also try beginning the explanation earlier in the book, revealing odd bits and pieces of the mystery as the plot proceeds.

Alternatively, consider writing the novel described in the explanation instead.

Now with 20% More Homily!

*Where the author tells us what
he's just spent 300 pages telling us*

And so, Jack reflected, it ended here. He surveyed the once thriving metropolis from high atop the twisted, smoking remains of Ergodraulics Tower. Far below him, he saw motion amid the rubble. Throughout the city, the children crawled out of basements and bomb shelters, walked blinking into the sunlight from the meat lockers and bank vaults that had protected them from the worst of it.

No, Jack thought, man was not meant to combine ergonomics and hydraulics without sufficient government regulation, and this was the result; but he had learned his lesson, and look there, look at the children. It was the indomitable human spirit.

He shook his fist at the heavens and thought, Yes, it was you who averted the final, final catastrophe that would have doomed us all, but—and here he pointed down to the games of ringo-levio and double dutch and kick-the-cat breaking out among the children all over the city—it's that spirit that will make us go on, make us build anew, build bigger, build better, explore new ideas in both ergonomics *and* hydraulics!

He leaned back against a crumpled girder and stared into the setting sun.

Yes, man had never given up, and never would. Since the day the first men stood up beneath the hot sun of the African plain, it had been ever forward, and whatever posture problems their upright stance would bring them, man would face, and struggle with, and someday conquer.

He might have been ashamed to be a Bilge of Bilge Hydraulics when this all started, but now he was proud— proud to be part of his family, proud to be his father's son, but more than that, proud to be a part of the family of man, man who, no matter what the odds . . . (and so on)

Sometimes, instead of a prologue that presents all the philosophical points the author will attempt to make, we are given at the end of a book a long monologue that explains to us all the philosophical points he has just attempted to make. Needless to say, we know. We were standing right there.

Fortunately, this final chapter is almost always extraneous to the story and can simply be lopped off.

PART II

—

CHARACTER

"How can people hate me," Tonio wondered, "when I'm buff, rich, and have every album Dylan ever made, on vinyl?"

Perhaps, after all your efforts to sabotage the plot, you think your novel might still be a little compelling. Your next best bet is to populate it with boring, unbelievable, and unpleasant characters. So who lives in Unpublished Novelville?

Many of its most prominent citizens have no traits at all. They go through the motions of the plot with the vacancy of bored minimum-wage employees. Even the protagonist has all the depth of a sock with a face drawn on it in magic marker. If the plot does not concern the workplace, none of the characters ever has to go to work. If the story doesn't center on a love affair, their world is populated by celibates. Their age is a matter of guesswork, and their class and ethnicity are absent, presumed "normal." We're told that the hero is uncovering a spy ring while romancing a gorgeous marine biologist at the bottom of the ocean—but he remains a sock puppet uncovering a spy ring of sock puppets at the bottom of a sock puppet ocean, etc.

Other characters are given heaps of personality, all of it bad.

They whine about their spouses, neglect their kids, and spend pages plotting revenge for a petty slight committed against them in the distant past. Or they ride a custom Harley and are intimately familiar with the capitals of Europe, but have no visible means of support. In the worst-case scenario, they are a budding actress named Rain Weste, and their best friend is Proudtail Pussy Weste, their rather exceptional cat.

Bad guys kill, torture, and maim with improbably sadistic glee. "I smirk at your pain!" the villain exults over the dying infant; meanwhile, back at Knockers, luscious featured dancer Lavish Rivers, who apparently has only two qualities that the author notices, finds herself irresistibly drawn to Dirk Tool, bland software programmer by day, bland software programmer who wandered into Knockers by night.

There are many tried and true ways of making characters uninteresting, unsympathetic, and lifeless. We cannot claim to be comprehensive. But any of the following approaches should be enough to terminate interest in every man, woman, and child in your novel.

4

CHARACTER ESSENTIALS

Joe had a really interesting personality.

One of the simpler tasks the author faces is saying *what Joe looks like*. In the hands of the dedicated unpublished author, even this becomes a chance to flounder. Passages jam-packed with words remain impressively description free. With the techniques below, you too can master the Zen of speaking without saying.

The Man of Average Height

Where characters are described in generic terms

Some descriptions of characters sound like a police report:

Joe was a medium-sized man with brown hair and brown eyes.

Alan wore a white shirt and blue jeans on his tall frame.

Melinda had a nice body and a pretty face.

Descriptions like these make your characters feel like stick figures. No one thinks of himself as a brown-haired man of average
height. Police-report description in general will be received by
the reader much as if it read "Horace was a man with two legs,
two arms, and a head on the top."

A blunder we have seen more than once recently is when
authors, reacting against the plethora of "large-breasted" girls
in fiction, describe a heroine as having "medium-sized breasts."
This amounts to saying she had breasts.

If you're going to tell us something about a character, tell us
something that we wouldn't have assumed on the basis of species
and gender. Err on the side of specificity. Novels are seldom
rejected because the characters are described too well. Try to concentrate on features and qualities that are specific to your character,
or if your character is in fact average, describe those features in a *way*
that is specific to your character, a way that suggests her personality. ("Marianne *detested* the way she didn't stand out in a crowd.")

What Color Am I?

*Where the character must be
in front of a mirror to know what she looks like*

Melinda paused to inspect herself in the mirror. A girl
with a nice body and a pretty face stood reflected there,
with medium-sized breasts that stood up proudly in her
halter top. She gave her long straight cinnamon hair a
perky toss and decided Joe would be crazy to let her go.

The reader wants to know what your characters look like. But how
do you get your point-of-view character to rattle off his height,

weight, and skin tone? Easy! Frog-march him to the mirror!

Unfortunately, this is so obviously a convention of bad fiction that it might as well read, "Looking in the mirror, Joe saw a tall, brown-haired man, trapped in a poorly written novel."

When the reader looks in a mirror, what she notices is not the color of her hair and the size of her breasts; she notices the hair out of place, the misbuttoned shirt, the smudged lipstick. People don't notice what they see every day; they see what's different, and the reader, on some level, will balk.

Making a character think about his own looks is not that difficult. Reminders are all around us. Any encounter with the opposite sex could reasonably cause a character to reflect—knowledgeably—on his own appearance. At best, the mirror is an unnecessary detour, because the point-of-view character whom you have dragged there already knows what he looks like. He could relay this information to the reader just as easily from the comfort of the couch.

A related problem is:

The Kodak Moment

As previous, with photo

As he passed the mirror, Joe noticed the blond hair and square-jawed features that had always won him attention from the girls. Then he saw, wedged in the mirror's corner, a photo of Melinda. Her pretty face was lusciously framed by long straight cinnamon hair and medium-sized but perfectly shaped breasts.

As noted above, most people think about their own appearance on an hourly basis—with chagrin, with conceit, with a resolve to join a gym. Likewise, they think about other people's appearance almost as often as they think of those people, and without any visual aids. In most cases, a character's entrance is sufficient segue into a description; there is no need for the point-of-view character to *think* anything; she is seeing it.

If you are having trouble transitioning to a physical description, use one of the constant reminders of appearance that exist in real life. The character could imagine his boyfriend with desire; his mother, with concern for her health; his boss, with disgust.

Channeling the E! Channel

Where celebrities are the yardstick

When he was young, people said Mark looked like George Clooney.

She looked regal, like an actress of the thirties, like Tallulah Bankhead.

Melinda looked like a slightly darker Halle Berry.

This usually goes wrong because if you put a picture of George Clooney in your reader's head, preexisting impressions of George Clooney will drown out any character you attempt to attach to it. It is even worse to play the Julia-Roberts-plus-or-minus game (a shorter Julia Roberts, an ugly Julia Roberts, an Asian-American Julia Roberts) because the reader is now doing math in his head whenever he should be thinking about your character.

It is fine if your character looks like Julia Roberts, but when you tell us about her, *describe* Julia Roberts, don't just invoke her, and never, ever mention Julia Roberts.

The Joan Rivers Pre-Novel Special

Where clothing is given too much prominence

"Joe, meet Wanda," said the hostess. Joe looked at Wanda appreciatively. She was wearing a short blue dress with bows at the shoulders, and matching blue kitten-heel sandals. A thin silver necklace completed the ensemble. He liked her immediately. He shook her hand and felt her appraising look.

He was wearing his charcoal gray blazer with the narrow lapels, and a pale green shirt. His tie was olive with tan stripes, and his pants were narrow-cut, in a daring dark green. The shoes were black suede loafers. The socks were thin wool and also black. Wanda smiled at his outfit, feeling as if she had known him forever.

While description of a character's clothes can give clues to his character, it does not in itself constitute character. Unless you are writing a sex-and-shopping novel, there is no need to give a complete inventory of someone's outfit. A single item—black jeans, a flimsy halter top—will usually do the work. The well-chosen detail is always more effective than the exhaustive inventory.

5

GETTING TO KNOW YOUR HERO

. . . and if she were a vegetable? Canned beans!

So, before we start the hero on his series of adventures, we want to get to know a little more about him. What makes him tick? What are his strengths and weaknesses? Is he married; does he live on a space station; is he criminally insane?

Unpublished novelists, however, understand that there is more to a character than the interesting stuff.

The Average Day

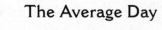

Where mundane detail fails to bring a character to life

Joe woke at seven and toasted an onion bagel, slathering it with cream cheese. He read the *Wall Street Journal* while eating his breakfast, then headed out to his Lexus to drive at an illegal 65 miles an hour to the gym. He did some cardio first, then lifted weights, working on his pectorals and triceps.

After a quick refreshing shower, Joe left the gym and got to work just five minutes late. Like every morning, he said "Howdy" to the secretary, who, as she always did, laughed and said "You scamp!" He went into his office and began his routine of blah while he admired the same view of blah blah that was just the same as every other day on which blah and like clockwork blah blah until it began to seem as if life was a empty series of meaningless actions.

This scene typically continues for three pages, covering every item in Joe's daily routine, from the banter with the guy at the newspaper stand to his favorite Chinese take-out food. The Average Day can result from one of two things. The first is the genuine desire to convey a life in all its manifold, pullulating detail. The other is the writer's idea that Joe's daily routine reveals his character. But few things give less insight into a man's soul than that he has toast for breakfast instead of the poached eggs.

The result, in both cases, is like reading a stranger's long to-do list. If the reader is exceptionally unlucky, Joe has a girlfriend, who also has a routine. The cure for the Average Day is simple: cut to the chase (see Part I).

The Child Is Father to the Digression

Wherein too much is made of a character's childhood

Joe's mother was a beautiful meteorologist, that his father had swept away after a whirlwind courtship. By the time Joe came along, though, their love had turned to hate, and there were always raised voices in his parents' bedroom late at night. As Joe grew up, he began to associate the fear he felt during their screaming matches with the idea of marriage. Perhaps that was the reason, he thought, putting

his sandals on and looking down the beach where Betty
was coming in from her swim, that he couldn't commit.
Little did she suspect that this innocent beach trip would
summon up ghosts of love betrayed. Poor Betty! How
could she ever understand the tangled web of his childhood?

The author now dives more deeply into Joe's troubled past, out-
lining the embarrassments of his first sexual experience and
detailing Joe's reaction to his grandma's death from a tragic
bookmobile accident. All this is meant to explain what makes
Joe the way he is: it is a tour of Joe.

The reader, however, is not baffled by the riddle of why guys
don't commit. Or why anyone might be neurotic, angry, shy, or
[add your own adjective here]. The author is also in danger of
going fractal—if we must know that Joe fears raisins because
of an unfortunate incident on a camping trip with his father and
the parish priest, shouldn't we know what made them the sort of
men who would do that with a raisin?

Characters can certainly be provided with some history. But
the relationship between that history and their behavior should
be more complex than Pavlovian dog psychology. And, generally,
unpublished authors are far more intrigued by their characters'
backstory than their readers are.

Too Good to Be True

*Wherein an attempt to make
the protagonist sympathetic overshoots the mark*

Melinda suppressed a grimace of concern as she saw the
homeless beggar on the subway stairs. Was five dollars

enough? She decided it would have to be; she still had her sister to support, and her mother might need that heart operation. How she wished she could work even longer hours, though the work was grueling. Melinda tried to keep the other girls' spirits up, always ready with a joke or a kind remark. "I don't know what we'd do without you," Esmerelda was always saying in her Salvadoran accent. All the women on the assembly line would nod in agreement.

Perfect people are boring. Perfect people are obnoxious because they're better than us. Perfect people are, above all, too good to be true.

Protagonists should only be as nice as everyday people are in real life. Making them nicer than the average reader will earn the reader's loathing, or make her laugh in disbelief.

An unprincipled gold digger who gives twenty dollars to a beggar is enchanting. A crusading human rights lawyer who volunteers at an animal shelter and also pauses on his way to court to give twenty dollars to a beggar makes us gag.

The Reader Will Not Like Your Hero Just Because

- He meditates
- He is in the middle of reading your own favorite authors
- He listens to your favorite bands and knows the liner notes

- He is a frustrated writer/artist/singer-songwriter
- He drives a quaint vintage car, which he has named
- He can whip up an amazing omelet from quirky ingredients
- He has green eyes
- He can sure hold his liquor
- He never touches the stuff
- He lives in a state of bohemian disorder
- He goes to Burning Man
- He stopped going to Burning Man when "they went commercial"
- Although he is a longshoreman, he shows a remarkable love of Art
- Although he is a classical pianist, the longshoremen accept him as a regular guy
- His maid is
    a: like a best friend
    b: an unpaid consultant in his detective business
- His grandma is the coolest person he has ever known

The Vegan Viking

Wherein the author accessorizes with politics

The knight Rogaine scratched his chin and pondered what the lovely Indinavir had said. She appeared not to accept the limited role of wife and mother that society had scripted for her. Rogaine himself had often mused that women were the cleverer sex. His mother was a wise woman who knew all the uses of the herbs, and had taught him to respect the ways of the dark-skinned sailors who came to their shores, whose matriarchal culture involved respect for all creatures, and whose ships were furnished with a loving attention to what was called, in the Eastern tongue, Feng Shui.

Fictional characters have politically correct or New Age values with much greater frequency than people in real life. This is especially unsuccessful when the character, as above, is living in a distant time and/or place, where the attitudes represented simply did not exist. (This is not a swipe at liberals; a novel by a right-winger featuring serfs musing about the importance of free-market incentives would be equally indigestible.)

A related issue is the recent vogue for gay characters in historical novels. Fine, we say, but do not use this as a way to demonstrate your other characters' tolerance, *which they would not feel*. Also refrain from remarks about the gay samurai's mincing walk or interest in clothes.

Love Me, Love My Cat

Wherein there is a cat

Mr. Whiskerbottom pattered out of his favorite lair beneath the sofa and meowed inquisitively. Melinda said, "Does His Highness want his dinner?" His Royal Pussliness seemed to squint his eyes in approval, his whole demeanor saying that he was a pampered potentate of the domestic realm. His fluffy tail swished back and forth in the air, and his cute tufted ears were slightly back with impatience. "I live to serve," Melinda laughed.

In most novels, a pet should have about as high a profile as an armchair. Unless it is a cat mystery, or the ferret or pot-bellied pig plays an important role in the plot, they can probably vanish from the story. Most of all, it does not work to give a character a pet to make him or her sympathetic. People are often at their *least* sympathetic when cooing over a bored cat. Unless the pet is a main character—the one who's really solving all those crimes—cut it down to one sentence, or delete.

If There Must Be a Cat, Do Not for the Love of God Name It . . .

- Magnifi-cat or similar pun
- after a composer (Bartok, Mahler, etc.)
- after a writer (Hemingway, Gertrude Stein, etc.)
- after an ancient Greek
- Mr. + adjective + anatomical feature (e.g., Mr. Prickly Paws)
- with two or more words, all starting with the same letter (Prickly Paws again)
- with any name plus the surname of the cat's owner (Bartok Finkelstein)
- with any name reflecting the owner's pride in his/her ethnic heritage or political leanings (Seamus, Rosa Parks, Trotsky, etc.)

Compassion Fatigue

Wherein the character is beyond help

Ever since Melinda Spew had given up college to look after her ailing mother, she had struggled with depression. All her friends had told her to just let her mother take care of herself. After all, Mrs. Spew was an alcoholic, who had shown Melinda nothing but brutality and let a series of drunken "stepfathers" use the growing girl to sate their angers and lusts. But Melinda couldn't cut the ties that bound her to her miserable past. And now that her mother had died, leaving her with crushing debt, Melinda was struggling just to survive. She had hoped the antidepressants prescribed by her psychiatrist would make her capable of work, like other people, but instead, she just gained 150 pounds.

Characters should have serious problems. But one character should not have every serious problem known to mankind. That doesn't mean your characters must be successful, beautiful, and content with life. Readers can identify with a protagonist who is a geek or a failure, but when all that character does is fail and wallow, identification becomes an unwelcome burden.

A pimply, lonely boy who's flunking out of school and gets beat up every day on the way home . . . well, who wants to see him get beat up one more time, with no hope in sight? However, if the same boy meets a mysterious stranger who promises him the Secrets of Power in Chapter One, readers will stick around to see the bullies get their comeuppance in Chapter Ten.

I Am Expressing My Sexuality

Wherein the character's sexual nature
overwhelms his other qualities

Joe gaped as the secretary bent over the wastebasket, her skirt tightening across her luscious ass. He was going to have to beat his meat later on, he knew. God! How could one guy be so horny?! He thought of the new *Hustler* magazine he had at home, which had already seen more use than most guys' girlfriends.

Heroes should not masturbate or ogle strangers in the first three chapters. Readers understand that people have sexual needs, but if the first thing they see are those needs, they will just think your character is gross. It's not that the reading public is uptight or moralistic; they know everybody masturbates, has unworthy thoughts about the buttocks of colleagues, etc. The reader also knows everyone poos. But if the first thing a character does is poo in front of the reader, the reader will think of him as the Pooing Character forevermore.

There are special circumstances where the hypersexual hero/heroine works. It works for James Bond and the heroines of Jackie Collins novels, for example: here the attraction is always mutual, promiscuity is normal, and that's part of the fantasy that sells the book.

There are also works by authors like Philip Roth and Martin Amis, which focus, usually comically, on the psychological travails of the protagonist, exploring his sexual obsessions. But these are, first of all, works of highbrow literature, so if you are not a writer of highbrow literature, you have made a wrong turn. This material is also spectacularly difficult, combining two advanced techniques that are each themselves difficult: sex scenes and humor (see Part VI, "Special Effects and Novelty Acts—Do Not Try This at Home", page 225). The beginning novelist can expect results similar to those of the novice skier who chooses to make his initial run on Widow-Maker Mountain while simultaneously attempting to sharpen knives for the first time.

Also, while it might be the writer's job to boldly explore the darker corners of his inner world, if what he finds there turns out to be a species that has evolved nowhere else, not only will readers fail to identify with the character to whom it is assigned, they will be drawn out of the story and into speculations about the author's participation in whatever bizarre behavior he has proposed.

6

SIDEKICKS AND SIGNIFICANT OTHERS

*"I love you more than any woman I've met
on the Upper West Side in a really long time."*

So your protagonist is a stick figure or—better still!—downright
repellent. Now let's turn to filling her world, and her bedroom,
with caricatures and bores.

Jimbo Knows Me Better
Than I Know Myself

*Wherein a friend character is
introduced to no purpose*

The phone rang and Melinda ran to get it. It was her best
friend, Jonquil.

"Hey, Monster-Mel," Jonquil greeted her old friend.

"Oh, Jonkey," Melinda cried delightedly. "I haven't
heard from you in two days!"

"I know, it's unusual for us to go so long without talking," said Jonquil. "You're the kind of person who really likes a lot of intimacy."

"Yes, but it shows me I've been withdrawn lately."

"Oh, you'll get back in your stride. I know you've been down in the mouth about this job. Maybe what you need is a Jonkey Junket."

Melinda thought about how many times Jonquil had boosted her spirits with one of these junkets. Melinda had always been the quiet, sometimes awkward one of the pair, while Jonquil was the outgoing party girl. Jonquil would take her to the top of the Empire State Building; or to eat at their favorite Italian restaurant ever, Gotti's; or sometimes they would just get a chick-flick on DVD and eat Ben & Jerry's Chubby Hubby ice cream in front of the television set. What would she have done all these years without Jonquil?

Typically, the above is five pages long and includes many cheerful exchanges to make sure the reader really gets the cheerful flavor of Jonquil and Melinda's exchanges. Melinda tells a long story about a previous good time they had, having apparently forgotten the fact that Jonquil was there. The Jonkey Junket takes place, and the reader is assaulted with a list of all the places the girls went, the items they purchased, and the colorful drinks they consumed.

If it is Joe on a Jimbo Junket, the boys will go to a game and order pizza—or they will be shown doing something *other* than watching sports, to demonstrate that they are not your typical guys.

Even worse is when Jonquil is succeeded by Maggie, who is succeeded by Ursula—because Melinda has more than one friend! And each friend shows a totally different side of Melinda!

Alternatively, there is

The Clone Entourage

Wherein friend characters proliferate into
_____*an indistinguishable mass*

After work, Buddy decided to stop by Eddie's place to see what the guys were up to. He parked and let himself in; they'd all be down in the rec room watching the game, no doubt.

He walked down the stairs and found everybody sitting around, watching the game.

"Hey, guys," Buddy said, and helped himself to a beer from the well-stocked fridge.

"Buddy!" Ralphie called out from across the room.

"Good to see you, Buddy," said Eddie, looking his way.

"Hey, Buddy," Billy said, holding up a hand, without taking his eyes off the TV.

"Anyone need another beer?" Buddy asked.

"I'll take one," Ralphie said.

"Me, too," said Eddie, and caught the one Buddy threw his way.

"Yeah, I could use one, too," said Billy.

Buddy settled in on the couch . . . another weekend had begun.

If the protagonist is going to have more than one friend, they should serve more than one purpose and have more than one personality. Most crucially, they must be distinguishable by more than the names that have been assigned to them. Generally, if they can collectively be referred to as "the guys," "the gals," or "the gang" with no harm to the plot, there doesn't need to be more than one of them.

Beyond a certain point (the point at which these encounters advance the plot) Buddy and Melinda need to choose between having friends and having a publishing deal.

The Cheerleader

Wherein a sidekick exists solely to admire the hero

"I'll really miss you when I go, Melinda," said Ephemera, the temp. "These seven hours we've spent together have been the most fun I had in a long time. Temping sucks."

"Oh, do you kiss your mother with that mouth?" Melinda joked.

Ephemera took a second to get it, then erupted in gales of laughter. Her eyes gleamed with mirth and admiration as she said, "Such a pretty girl, and a sense of humor too!"

"Yeah, but it is too bad you have to go back to the temping twilight zone," Melinda said.

"The temping twilight zone! You say such witty things—your talents are really wasted in this office."

"Oh, I'm pretty happy here," Melinda said. "Anyway, no peace for the wicked."

The temp sighed appreciatively. "Wow, that's so true," she said. "I never looked at it in quite that way before."

"And you can often do more good in humble surroundings."

"Wow, you're right. I have a feeling this conversation is going to change my view of things forever."

The author here is replacing actual witty or profound remarks from the protagonist with a bit character who is so easily impressed that she appears mildly psychotic. This is a subtle instance of "The Underpants Gnomes": the author knows what kind of person she wants the character to be, but she is not doing the work to get the reader from here to there. Making another character laugh louder does not make the dialogue funnier. Characters like this often have the same relationship to the "Onanism" plot that blow-up dolls do to actual onanism.

The writer here has two options: she can work harder, or she can allow that the character is only as clever and funny as the character actually is.

The Faceless Multitude

Wherein numerous extras are introduced and discarded

When she got to the picnic, Nell's brother Alex came forward first, giving her a warm hug with his strong Irish arms. Over his shoulder, she could see her cousins Max, Betty, and Lucy, with her second cousin, also named Lucy, and their Great Dane, also named Max. "Good to see you," Alex said, letting her go. She stood back, grinning widely. Alex lived in Delaware, and it was always good when he came to town.

"Mom, Dad," Nell called out when she saw them. They waved and headed toward her but were waylaid by Mitzi, Bitsy, and Ramona, triplets on her father's side.

> Nell sure did love the big family picnics that they had every summer. It almost made her forget her job as a homicide detective in the worst part of Baltimore, but not quite. The McQuiver case haunted her even now, and tomorrow, when she was back at her desk . . .

In real life, people are often close with their family and spend time with them whenever they can. If you would like to think of your character as that type of person, please be our guest. But be a considerate guest. When we invite someone into our home, we do not expect that person to bring the entire family with them. Unless somebody actually figures into your plot, we do not need to meet the person. Like a small business, a novel cannot afford to carry dead weight, even if it is a close family member.

It is likewise unnecessary to introduce a mother and/or father into the narrative—usually through the medium of a long telephone call on the subject "How's things?"—to demonstrate that the protagonist does, like all mammals, have parents.

Love-Interest Barbie

Wherein love is skin deep

> Joe let his eyes linger on her bright blue eyes, her perfectly tanned skin, her long blonde hair. Melinda could have been a model—if it weren't for the largeness of her perfectly shaped breasts. Her arms were slender and golden, her legs were long and shapely. She looked like a cross between Scarlett Johansson and Angelina Jolie—only better. Joe didn't think he'd ever been so much in love.

Many love interests are skin deep. With male characters, "cobalt blue eyes" are a telltale symptom; in female characters, beware of "long blonde tresses." In a movie, when Scarlett Johansson appears, and the male lead instantly falls for her, we see why. In a novel, we see the same typeface we've been seeing all along. The most impassioned, eloquent description of Angelina Jolie naked will not have the impact of five seconds of poorly shot video; and while millions of years of evolution might have programmed us to respond to size, it is not font size. Worse, without such instinctive responses, we are all too likely to resent characters—even of the opposite sex—for being ideally gorgeous. This doesn't mean your love interests shouldn't be good-looking, only that they must also have a lovable quality. At the very least, they should have a quality.

Remember: blonde, brunette, and redhead are not personality types.

Men Are from Cliché; Women Are from Stereotype

Wherein the characters are built solely of broad gender stereotypes

Melinda picked up Joe's beer-stained sports section with a wry smile, replacing it with another saccharin-berry scented candle. As she sat on the pouffe to enjoy her copy of *Brides' Shoe Monthly,* she wondered if he would remember to call for their third-date anniversary.

Meanwhile, across town, Joe gave the jailbait waitress a sly wink, letting the caveman in him take over. He'd taken advantage of Melinda's absence to order the Surf 'n' Sty Fry with extra cholesterol. At any moment, Dick would arrive for a fun-filled night of brewski-fueled male bonding. God damn if Joe didn't love that old hooligan, though of course he'd never tell him so.

This love affair is set up as a war of sexist clichés. She is always saying "Let's talk"—*the most dreadful words a man can hear!* He'd rather be watching the game, and that is his sole personality trait. The odd observation about gender difference is fine, but your characters should have a greater divergence from stereotype than your average beer commercial.

In real life, couples bond and war over a million different things. The causes of divorce are like beautiful, unique snowflakes. Give some thought to the possible history of your characters' love affair, the things they do together, their inside jokes. With a little investment of time, you can draw a relationship individual enough for people to care about, and that the editor considering your novel didn't see last week in a stand-up routine on Comedy Central.

Prince Charming Doesn't Deserve Me

Wherein the bad boyfriend is more sympathetic than the protagonist

Quickly Melinda recounted Joe's crimes to herself. He forgot the dry cleaning, didn't have fun at her office party, fell asleep right after sex that time, and clearly wasn't happy about helping with her mother's tax forms—on their third-date anniversary. Which she had to remind him of! And for which he bought her red roses, when he knew she only liked white roses! After that, she could hardly be blamed for her night of passion with the cobalt-blue-eyed folk singer, Jesse, Melinda thought, as she threw another armful of Joe's clothes out into the street.

This is the unworthy boyfriend of the protagonist, exemplifying everything that's wrong with men. Unless the reader is sane, in which case his fate exemplifies everything that's wrong with whiny divas. The just-okay boyfriend who gets turfed out for a better model often takes the reader's sympathies with him. The bad boyfriend has to be unequivocally bad—he gets drunk every night; he blows the heroine's money at the racetrack; he says those jeans *do* make her look fat. Above all, he cheats *first*; what she does after that doesn't feel like cheating.

Your protagonist can leave a nice-but-dull partner for a handsome stranger who "just feels like home," but she should do it with remorse, not vindictive glee.

The Lovely Prison Warden's Daughter

Wherein a love interest suddenly appears to patch a plot hole

Suddenly Joe perked up. Down the dank hallway came a shapely girl. It must be the daughter of the prison warden; what other girl would be caught dead in a jail after dark, when all the other staff were asleep? She caught his eye and smiled guiltily.

"Hey, gorgeous," he said.

"Are you talking to me?" She paused with a shy air. Then they both laughed.

"Well, I wasn't talking to Basher Jones, the psychopath incarcerated across from me! Anyway, he's conveniently asleep."

"Conveniently?" she purred. From the way she cocked her head, Joe knew it would be no time before the ring of keys on her juicy hip—and the delectable girl herself—were in his possession.

The flash-in-the-pan love interest as a solution to the hero's troubles is a useful trick in thrillers, mysteries, and simply to liven up a draggy passage in experimental fiction. (What would Virginia Woolf *be* without her prison-warden's-daughter scenes?) But writers must take the trouble to create the love interest some pages *before* the lovely prison warden's daughter (lovely bank teller, lovely plastic surgeon, lovely martial artist, what have you) acts on her headlong passion.

The Funny Valentine

Wherein the protagonist settles for less

Melinda surveyed Panky's saggy cheeks, his wrinkled Spock T-shirt, and his rosacea. She took his clammy hand in both hers and sighed. At last she saw past his stammer, his clumsiness, his pathological fear of moths, his nasal laugh, his elevator shoes, his job as circus geek, his body. Why couldn't she appreciate what was under her nose the whole time! All those nights they'd sat up discussing the problems she had with Lance, he'd been longing for her, she now realized. Pancreas Jones was always her best friend—could he be something more?

Readers love a comeback kid, and can appreciate that the protagonist is not shallow, but there are limits. The frog does have to turn into a prince before the wedding night. More subtle, but equally painful to the reader is the

Last Tango in Santa's Village

Wherein the love interest is a sexual zero

Melinda surveyed Santa's generous frame, his bright red suit, his snowy beard. She took his plump hand in both hers and sighed. At last she saw past superficialities to understand that it was Santa, with his warm and loyal heart, who was the real man—not cobalt-eyed, washboard-abbed Blade at all! Santa Claus was always her best friend—could he be something more?

No. Absolutely not. Under no circumstances. He cannot.

The cuddly best friend character may not be disgusting, but he does utterly lack sex appeal. In the many novels where he turns into the love interest by story's end, the novelist always puts him through a more-or-less subtle masculinization. This may be through ultrafine touches like having him move a sofa, manfully taking the heroine's side in a dispute when she's becoming tearfully desperate, or just making knowledgeable comments about football. Very subtle cues like this may be coupled with a make-over tactic like a flattering haircut and with altered emotions in the heroine, which slowly build over the course of a few scenes.

(Until recently, the feminine version of this character would have to give up a job, become misty-eyed about babies, and/or realize that Mr. Knightly knows best. Recent strides have brought her to a point where she has merely to lose ten pounds and learn to see her own inner beauty, as Raoul can.)

In the Santa example, suppose that as Melinda gets to know Santa better she learns that he's a former boxer who had to make tracks for the North Pole after some shady incident in which a man died. His real name is "Jared." Then, as his unspoken passion for her begins to take its toll, Santa begins to drop pounds and hit the whiskey. The smart red suit is replaced by torn jeans and an old sweatshirt. And just before the kiss that makes the lightbulb go on in Melinda's brain, Santa shaves.

It's not necessary to make the best friend into a stud. But he must be attractive on some level, not just safe. We get enough of that kind of compromise in real life.

The Road to the Trash Heap Is Paved with Good Intentions

"Write what you know" has never sat well with us, but we have seen far too many embarrassments result when writers stray too far from writing *who* they know.

Priscilla, Queen of the Clichés

The gay best friend is traditional, and handy too. Gay characters regularly provide male perspective; female perspective; a nonthreatening shoulder to cry on; comic mix-ups of romantic intent; and a demonstration of the main character's sophistication and open-mindedness.

Most of all, though, they are useful as a constant source of catty, campy, clever dialogue for comic relief. Unfortunately, many beginning writers seem to think that having established that their character is gay, the clever dialogue will show up on its own. They get no further than having him refer to men as "she" and women as "girlfriend" while making dismissive but nonspecific critiques of other characters' taste in clothing and interiors (*"BOR-*ing!").

Chief Politically Correct Eagle

This is the ethnic character who appears in the narrative solely to give the protagonist an opportunity to demonstrate liberal views on race. The character typically has no qualities apart from an ethnic identity, and no other role in the story. This is almost always glaringly obvious and tends to achieve results opposite those intended.

Some of My Best Friends . . .

Here the ethnic character is uncomfortably close to a racist stereotype, if not indistinguishable from a racist stereotype, if not (let's be honest) a racist stereotype. Worst is when the stereotype is combined with Chief Politically Correct Eagle in a single character. This results in things like a white character inspired to think approvingly about affirmative action by a black character whose dialogue reads like something lifted from Amos 'n' Andy. For peak ill effect, make the stereotyped character experience an unusual sense of bonding with the protagonist because he is one of the few of his kind who "gets it." ("You know what, Meester? You're all right.")

This is not unique to liberal white authors. If the

term "White Devil" both appears in your novel and fully describes any character, take note.

Think Globally, Shop Locally

A similarly unfortunate effect can result when you attempt to showcase a character's deep and humanitarian nature by bringing in a tragedy completely unrelated to the plot for her to reflect upon. ("A headline at the newsstand outside Bergdorf's caught Gloria's eye, and she paused there, overwhelmed with empathy for victims of the famine/tidal wave/war/other-tragedy-lately-in-the-news. Life was sad.") We salute your good intentions, but send them a check and get back to your story. Other people's tragedies, particularly when they're real, tend to make anything your character does seem irrelevant.

7

BAD GUYS

"Now that I have you in my power, I shall tell you my whole life story!"

Phew! We're done making the protagonist insufferable and the love interest uninteresting. Now let's turn to making the bad guy completely unbelievable. For antagonists sure to antagonize any editor out of buying your book, try some of the handy tricks below.

Inside the Mind of a Criminal

*Wherein the villain's evil-doings
are motivated by the desire to do evil*

Cruella sat at her onyx desk, idly pulling the wings off a fly, and thought about Joe. The weakling would do anything for that simpering daughter of his. Cruella had nothing but contempt for that sort of sentimentality. She had half a mind to engineer some "accident" to remove the brat once and for all. It would be diverting to see Joe's

misery—all the tears and fuss for nothing but a child!
Then the poor fool wouldn't have the strength to keep up
his optometry work—that sickeningly generous two-for-
one offer of contact lenses would be gone forever, leaving
legions of the poorest in darkness! Yes, an accident—just
like the one Cruella's own whining son had fallen victim
to so many years ago!

In creating foes, writers sometimes go to such extremes that the
bad guy exhibits a degree of nastiness to which the human race
has happily not yet evolved. These villains unselfishly dedicate all
their free time to plotting Mother Teresa's downfall, without any
cash incentive or reason to hate Mother Teresa other than "her
phony nice act makes me see red."

An antagonist should always be provided with a reason for his
actions that we can understand without ourselves being psycho-
paths. And in stories that are not about serial killers or monsters,
it is vital that the hero's business rival, difficult boss, or cheating
boyfriend should not be played by the Prince of Darkness.

Do not try, however, to address this problem with

But He Loves His Mother

*Wherein a villain is given
one good quality to round him out*

Shiv sniggered as he poked the prone body of his newest
recruit. She was prime meat. His clients would appreciate, as they always did, his skill at getting the youngest
girls around to work the streets to pay for his crack habit
and snuff film collection. This chick was probably just

out of junior high. Well, by the time she woke up she'd have more sexual experience than a lot of women twice her age. Then it was just a matter of keeping her locked in this cellar and injecting her with horse until she was hooked. Then they got real nice to old Shiv, yes-sir-ee.

Going to the sink to wash the blood from his hands, he spied the photo of his mother that held pride of place there. Immediately his face softened. Ma—that was a real woman. He remembered a more innocent time, when he used to work three paper routes to pay for her medication. If only she hadn't gone and died, maybe Shiv would have turned out to be a better man.

Sometimes, uncomfortably aware that the antagonist is turning into a caricature, the author tries to "round him out" by giving him a good side. Jack robs and cheats and beats his kids—but still pines after his first love. Adolf introduces Fascism to Germany, spreads war throughout Europe, murders millions in concentration camps—but he's a strict vegetarian and loves his dog. Tossing in a touching scene with his German shepherd Blondie and a dish of lentils won't make Hitler's character "balanced." Hitler's character *isn't* balanced. The only way to avoid caricature is the hard way: making the bad guy's insane behavior and motivations believable.

The Retirement Speech

Wherein the villain improbably recounts her evil deeds

"Now that it's all over, there won't be any harm in my explaining how I outsmarted you," Cruella said, sneering down the barrel of the gun she had trained on Joe's face. "First, I bribed the Commissioner and paid a certain unscrupulous rival optician to take care of your meddling mother. One amusing adjustment to the glaucoma test machine and—well, she never saw what hit her! Your secretary was the next to go. I suppose she must have been surprised to discover a tarantula instead of a paper jam when she opened up the photocopy machine! Then it was the turn of that silly prison warden's daughter you liked so much. The poor thing was no match for the rabid cougar I released in H block . . ."

"Carry on," Joe said with a comfortable grin, stroking the audio transmitting device he had concealed on his person.

Criminals in fiction often seem only to have stolen, kidnapped, murdered, and committed unspeakable sex acts with the child's beloved pet monkey because they are *so* looking forward to telling someone all about it. Try to find some more plausible way of revealing the villain's evil-doing.

Revenge Is a Dish Best Served in Public

When the author has failed to move on

"Just the reaction I expected from a wimp like you," Delilah sneered. "You'll never find another woman who'll put up with your martyr act. And now that I'm taking the kids—who, by the way, you'll never see again once I get through with the false pedophilia accusations—no one will ever love you."

Andy wiped the sweat from his brow. He couldn't believe Delilah would leave him for Rod Hardwick now, right after his cancer diagnosis. But a part of him that he didn't want to hear knew that it was because of the cancer diagnosis. Delilah never had any tolerance for weakness. His friends had tried to warn him that she was shallow, stupid, selfish, frigid, and had unattractive tree-trunk legs. But he wouldn't listen—he had been blinded by his warm and trusting nature.

Behind all this, the reader spies the fuzzy outline of the writer's last amour.

A Novel Called It

Wherein an abusive parent exists

"Melinda, you were always an idiot," Mr. Dobson sneered. "It's a good thing I stopped you from going to that job interview. Look at your stupid fat face! They would have laughed you out the door."

Melinda flushed but said nothing, continuing to mop up the beer her father had spilled. If only she could get up the courage to defy him. Staring into the puddle of beer, she seemed to see herself as a child—huddled in a ball while her drunken father took swings at her with an anvil. Though the blows made her see stars, she knew she had to endure it to protect her baby brother, Tiny Tim.

A sudden blow woke her out of her reverie. "Quit napping and get me another brewski," Mr. Dobson barked.

Bad parents are everywhere in unpublished fiction. Whole cities of abusive fathers and sneering mothers live in the pages of books that can't be sold. While occasionally, and notably in the horror genre, this sort of material can be made good (*Carrie*; V.C. Andrews), most cruel parents in fiction are just as much fun as they are in real life.

The Riddler

Wherein the nefarious plot is more complex than string theory

Yes, thought Brainiac, stroking his tarantula, Henri IV; now was the time to convince the Mayor he was telling the truth about the lies he had previously told, this time but not the last two times, except for the part about Joe and the daughter of the prison warden, unless the Mayor had not believed that before. The murders could be pinned on Cruella, whose fingerprints would be on the glaucoma test machine from the time he had carelessly tossed it to her (having himself worn gloves, *mieux de sic!*) with a waggish "Think fast!" Then there would just be time to plant a few bad numbers in the computer file containing Joe's research, so that X would appear to equal less than 5.3202—a figure that is not statistically significant! He laughed out loud at his diabolical cleverness.

Overly intricate schemes of the villain can read like knotty tax litigation. If the reader can't understand your plot, he won't enjoy it. If he is faced with the dilemma of deciding whether he is stupid or your book is stupid—well, we know how we'll bet, because we are not stupid.

While a surprise revelation about the villain's plans can be a wonderful twist, it will lose its thrill if understanding it requires advanced calculus. And it should never be more complex than the entire surrounding plot (see "The Manchurian Parallax of the Thetan Conspiracy Enigma," page 48).

I'm Melting!

Wherein the villain conveniently gives up

Pierce laughed as his grip tightened on Melinda's wrist. He leered at Santa grotesquely, apparently enjoying the bound-and-gagged man's yelps of pain.

"So, you thought you could just leave me for Big Red there, huh?" he jeered to Melinda. "Think again!"

He was about to tear her blouse open and sate his lust in front of Santa's helpless gaze. How could Melinda ever have found his brutish advances appealing? But suddenly, Santa burst free of his bonds, having figured out the knot somehow. He tore the tape from his mouth, divesting himself thereby of his beautiful but unsexy full white beard. After a brief gasp of pain, the red-faced Santa shouted, "Let her go, or you'll be sorry!"

"Aw," Pierce said, letting Melinda's arm go and shrugging nervously. "I didn't mean anything. No need for anyone to get hurt."

Often, at the key moment of confrontation, the villain suddenly collapses, seemingly tuckered out by all his energetic villainy.

The good guys, having been helpless to defeat the antagonist for 200 pages, now poke him gently and he obligingly deflates, seemingly aware that this is the climax of the book, and that's his job.

This is true not only of climactic scenes. Avoid fight scenes at any point in the book in which the bad guy falls in a heap at the first blow from the protagonist.

The Fearless Exposé

Wherein a novel is populated by straw men

Victor pulled his car into the driveway and was instantly assaulted by the smells and sounds of his new neighbor's feminist "lifestyle." Hard-working and stoic, Victor had not complained, had even insisted on tolerance at the last meeting of the block association. He wished they'd wear some clothes, though, he thought, as he walked around to his back door, a trip that gave him a clear view of their entire backyard. As usual, she'd invited more of her kind over to chant naked and burn pictures of presidents while their fatherless children ran neglected and ignored about the yard with matted and unwashed hair and diapers in need of a change.

Unnoticed by the angry women, who were cackling gleefully around the fire, one of the children was toddling dangerously close to the edge of the swimming pool. Victor rushed across the yard, getting there just in time to stop the child from falling in.

"Whoa, there, little fella," Victor said, scooping up the adorable tyke.

"Get your filthy patriarchal hands off my child," his new neighbor shrieked as she ran toward him.

"But—"

"I know what you wanted to do to him," she said as she snatched the child out of his arms. She put the boy down and pushed him toward some of the other children. "Go and play, and remember to be ashamed of your penis."

Authors sometimes use the bad guy as an opportunity to vent about a despised group or belief. It is best to keep the editorializing from getting too heavy-handed, or your character will read like a walking mission statement. Please feel free to make your bad guy a neocon, a teenager with no manners, or a passionate Zionist—but try to avoid implying that this is the thing that makes him bad.

Pop Quiz

Which would be most likely to fit a character in your novel?

I. "Girlfriend, that look is *fierce* on you!" said

    A. Bruce, the stylist, with a lisp.

    B. Oprah.

    C. the child, posing in front of a mirror in her Mommy's shoes.

    D. ZORM, the ship computer.

II.   Revealing his nefarious plot, he spoke

    A. in a German accent.
    B. German.
    C. germanely.
    D. to his hand puppet, Popo.

III. When he came home from college, his mother had

    A. fresh-baked chocolate chip cookies ready on a plate for him.
    B. kept his room exactly the way it was when he had left.
    C. moved without telling him.
    D. turned into a carnivorous plant.

IV.   The teenager took

    A. our burger order.
    B. a gateway drug.
    C. umbrage at the teacher's assertions about the Balkan situation.
    D. his turn flensing the giant.

V.   The pretty secretary batted

    A. her eyelashes.
    B. away the cheeky executive's hand.
    C. .320 as the starting shortstop.
    D. ineffectually at the lustful rhino.

VI. **The eight-year-old child wept**

    A. every time his parents fought downstairs.

    B. as the priest took his wicked pleasure.

    C. when the remote control was wrestled from his sticky paw.

    D. for the next five years, pausing only to adjust the device.

VII. **The old lady gasped**

    A. at the strong language of the men.

    B. with joy at the news of the armistice.

    C. with pleasure as he rammed it home.

    D. "ZORM, you flatterer!"

VIII. **The powerfully built CEO made**

    A. love to his secretary.

    B. $10 million on stock options.

    C. latkes.

    D. porcupines cry at the sheer beauty of his voice.

IX. **The young hairdresser turned out to be**

    A. gay, just like Bruce!

    B. on the talkative side.

    C. the very man to ask about all things botanical.

    D. blind as a bat.

X.   The businesswoman never had enough time

    A. for her children.

    B. to have children.

    C. to properly bury the children.

    D. to buy a cell phone, which she came to
        regret when trapped in her bathroom
        by the alien lizard-creature.

XI. In her childhood, the lesbian

    A. had been sexually abused.

    B. liked to play with trucks, not dolls.

    C. had a crush on her pretty aunt.

    D. made porcupines cry with the sheer beauty
        of her knitting.

SCORING

A. 5 points

B. 4 points

C. 2 points

D. 0 points

40–55: Your characters are all unimaginative stereotypes. Sure to offend anyone who belongs to the group represented, these are not based on people; they are based on bad fiction, which was itself based on slightly less bad fiction.

30–40: You are suffering from a bad case of predictability. While your characters are not exactly cardboard, they are the thing right next to cardboard. Maybe balsa wood, except that balsa wood has uses.

20–30: You are hitting a reasonable balance for most forms of commercial fiction. While somewhat familiar, these characters are interesting enough to hold the reader's attention without making them wonder what the author's parents did to him. Keep it up, smarty pants!

10–20: If you are writing a work of psychological complexity, kooky comedy, or alien possession, you are still within the safe zone. Otherwise, try to be less creative.

0–10: You have confused clever with annoying. Irresponsible friends will tell you you're funny and daring, leading you to believe that all those rejections slips are due to your "shocking" "originality."

PART III

—

STYLE—THE BASICS

*Amazingly, Bob's awesome sentences conveyed
no information at all!*

Of all known ways of killing an editor's interest in your book, style is the swiftest and deadliest: the literary equivalent of a fast-acting poison. While a tiresome plot and wooden characters may take paragraphs or even pages to kill an editor's interest, a droning or inarticulate voice can put a stop to all reading in a single sentence.

Many achieve this simply by not paying attention to the language they are using as they write. Zipping along, strewing infelicities in their wake, these writers apparently believe that second drafts are for sissies. Hours of labor on a single paragraph, however, need not put incomprehensibility out of reach. Some will find their hard work rewarded with the removal of every last trace of meaning.

If you're serious about staying unpublished—for the love of God, *misuse long vocabulary words*. A single well-misplaced "erogenous" or "funicular" can annihilate all threat of publication. Where a simple descriptive word will do, don't use it. People should "emanate" from rooms; ideas should "permeate" heads. If you have the nerve, the idea can emanate the head, and the people can permeate from rooms. Never stop short at the point where meaning is merely unclear; remember, context might still permit the reader to interpret the sentence.

Do not ever trust your reader to understand that a weeping character is sad. Explain it, preferably in the language of an anthropologist's field notes. *She now experienced sadness. He underwent grief.* When in doubt, use psychobabble. Any threat of emotional resonance in a scene can be averted by the application of words like "dysfunctional" or "commitment-phobic." In fact, jargon of many types can be useful. If you know any obscure whaling terms, or terminology used only by Dungeonmasters in the mid-eighties, it sure would be a waste not to put them in your novel.

As long as a cliché is available, don't waste your time making up your own images—you've got a novel to write! If you *must* exercise your powers of invention, be sure the image you create is bizarre or inappropriate. A stream should gush over the rocks "with the force of a young man's urine." A passionate man should make love to his wife "like Khrushchev at the UN."

Style is a complicated thing, and all these directives may seem overwhelming. But with the simple, step-by-step demonstrations that follow, you, too, can learn to create prose that is at once meaningless, leaden, and impenetrable.

8

WORDS AND PHRASES

Brandy? Vouchsafe errant couch! CRANBERRIES! CRANBERRIES!

Fiction is made of language and language is made of words. Writers have long appreciated words for their ability to communicate ideas to readers. Some writers, though, seem unaware that this works only when both parties agree beforehand on what words mean. Overlook this simple but essential precondition, and things can go wrong in a number of ways.

The Puffer Fish

Wherein the author flaunts his vocabulary

His father was IRA and his mother was Quebecois, and they had relinquished their mortal coils in the internecine conflagration that ended their conjoined separatist movement, IRA-Q. The appellation he was given by his progenitors was Ray O'Vaque ("Like the battery," he'd elucidate, with an adamantine stare that proscribed any mirth). In his years of incarceration, however, he had earned the sobriquet "Uncle Milty" for his piscine amatory habits.

He had been emancipated from the penitentiary for three weeks, and now his restless peregrinations had conveyed him to this liminal place, seeking compurgation in the permafrost of the hyperborean tundra, which was an apt analogue of the permafrost in his heart. He insinuated himself into the caravansary with nugatory expectations, which were confirmed by the exiguous provisions for comfort. But then the bartender looked up from laving the begrimed bar, his eyes growing luminous as he ejaculated, "Milt!"

Beginning writers often believe that the true genius uses only words from the furthest reaches of the English language, the darkest recesses of the dictionary, the sort of words that cannot survive on their own in any natural environment.

Sorry; this is not writing. This is showing off, and nobody likes a show-off.

There are of course things you would write that you would not say in conversation ("I said, bewildered"), but words that draw attention to themselves by their rarity draw attention away from the story you are telling and remind the reader of the writer and his thesaurus. In a worst-case scenario, a game of ping-pong develops between the writer's thesaurus and the reader's dictionary.

When the reader has stopped to wonder at your delamificatious vocabulary, or, worse, when the reader has stopped because the word you've used has no more meaning to him than a random ptliijnbvc of letters, the reader is not involved in your story.

This is not to say that you should write with one hand tied

behind your back, making sure that you only use language accessible to a fifth grader. There is nothing wrong with making the occasional reader occasionally reach for the dictionary. However, the only legitimate reason to do that is *if the word you have chosen is the best word to express the idea.* Generally, saying "edifice" instead of "building" doesn't tell your reader anything more about the building; it tells the reader that you know the word edifice.

The Crepuscular Handbag

Wherein the author flaunts somebody else's vocabulary

Henderson toyed with the onset of Melinda's bikini, ruminating his designs. "Asleep so soon?" he whickered. Of course he was vigilant that this sleep was the due of the unsavory drug he had slavered in her drink prior to the debarking of his private schooner boat. Ululating under his breath, he perused her bikini to the floor and embroiled himself in her well-endowed bust.

He vacated a myriad times in the naively prolonged girl. She didn't suspect a nary, lolling Michigan-style. "You will sell for pretty pennies," he voiced, palming her redolent hind.

Using words the reader does not know is a bad idea, but it is at least defensible; there are excuses. There are no excuses for using words you yourself do not know. Nonwriters might wonder how this could happen, and frankly, from time to time, so do we, but it does, and with appalling frequency.

If you've seen a word only once and have not taken the trouble to look it up, the chances of shooting yourself in the foot are high.

Using a word almost correctly, or using a word almost exactly like the right word, amounts to almost speaking English. You may think that the occasional slip-up won't matter; but the language you choose is the clothing in which your novel is draped, and saying "incredulous" when you mean "incredible" is the prose equivalent of walking into a meeting wearing your underwear on the outside.

We have no way of knowing what words you are going to misuse, so we cannot offer you a list. What we can offer, though, is a test that you yourself can apply to any word, whenever you are in doubt.

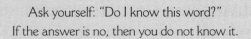

A Test: Do I Know This Word?

Ask yourself: "Do I know this word?"
If the answer is no, then you do not know it.

The short-term solution is to use a word you *do* know. That means a word you would comfortably use when talking to an overeducated and sarcastic friend who would not hesitate to make fun of you for misusing a word.

If you feel that limiting yourself to words you know leaves you with too small a vocabulary for your purposes, there is no short-term solution. Your only recourse is to take the time to read more books and to expand the kind of books you read. You may have fallen into the habit of reading only a few favorite authors, or reading only within a particular genre, or subgenre, of book.

By casting a wider net, you will catch more words, and your vocabulary will inevitably—though slowly—be enriched.

The Crepitating Parasol

Wherein the author trips over his own cleverness

Pausing in their circumambulation of the verdancy, the duo jocularly noted a bi-canine (that is, a duplication of Fidos, one perched atop deux) in 4/4-time venereal congress amid the rhododenra. The cadence of the connubial kinetics near-mesmerizing, the pooch performance secured the gawkery of Jasper and Jasperia.

"The rites of spring," quoted Homo Sapiens the first (for he was aware, in a trice, of that species he called his own, differentiating his bipedal egoism from the four-square unselfconsciousness of the curs). "Qua Stravinsky's well-known jeu d'esprit."

"Ah, scrumptuoso!" exulted his perky hominid companion-ette, humming a few bars. Her virile counterpart-ner now brought his attention to attention, however at ease, focused on the spectacle of her unvoluminous but perfectly formed mammary attractions. Truly the HS (Homo Sapiens) manifested too, sporadically, as dog.

Some writers feel compelled not only to wrangle exotic words but to make them do tricks as well. For these writers, no formation is too baroque; no pun is too obscure.

Nigel Tufnel of Spinal Tap memorably pointed out that there is a fine line between clever and stupid. The harder you try to be clever, the more momentum you will have when you arrive at that line, and the less likely you are to notice when you cross it.

Very skilled writers will sometimes use baroque prose to good effect, but even among successful literary authors, the vast majority avoid flowery writing. Writing is not like figure skating, where flashier tricks are required to move up in competition. Ornate prose is an idiosyncrasy of certain writers rather than a pinnacle all writers are working toward.

Trans-Parent

Authors often say that their novels are like their children, and you want your novel, just like your children, to reflect well on you. When it goes out into the world, you hope that it will make you proud. But like a parent, an author must learn that her novel has needs of its own, and they are not the same as the author's.

Yes, you want your son's behavior toward women to reflect a loving relationship with his mother. However, if a woman is compelled to think about that relationship whenever they're in bed together, something has gone very very wrong.

A humorous or ornately embroidered passage that takes the reader out of the novel to reflect on the author's brilliance is likely to be a bug, rather than a feature. In fact, whenever you are particularly taken with a bit of your own cleverness, it is not a bad idea to stop and consider whether it serves your novel or you.

Anything that draws attention to the author at the expense of her novel is bad parenting.

Are Sticks and Stones Still an Option?

Wherein the author mangles common expressions

Herbert Hooviér was the crème de la menthe of fashion reporters. He had spent six years honing his journalistic nose as a foreign correspondent first, and was pretty tough company to get past. Normally he wouldn't trust anyone with his back tied, and always made sure he looked before he took a leap of fate. But he had met his match made in heaven in Vera Wang, the fashionable designer.

She was as pretty as he pictured, with a body so great you could bounce her hindquarters off it. She was the apples and oranges of his eye. Herbert, or Herb, tried not to give in to his urgent, but she was a piece of no resistance, and his masculine whiles were no match for her cat's meow.

When she opened the door for their second date, she looked great, stunning him.

"Your place or mine?" she queried.

"Touché," he returned, begging her question.

When somebody is said to speak like a native, it means that person has learned to speak a language idiomatically. Conversely, when you use idioms incorrectly, it makes you sound as if you come from a different culture than the reader, and possibly a different planet. Getting individual words wrong can make you sound illiterate; getting idioms wrong can make you sound as if you don't speak English.

While you can't simply look these things up in a dictionary, you are fortunate to live in a time when you can google anything. If you have any uncertainty about an idiom, try an Internet search and see how other people have used it. If the phrase you are using does not return a few thousand hits, you probably have the wording of the idiom wrong.

And if you are thinking "I can't possibly check everything that way," perhaps you have too many such phrases. This can result in

Breeding Contempt

Wherein the author relies too much on clichés

She gave him a deep, melting kiss before falling into his strong arms, swept away by her feelings. Her mind was a whirlwind of conflicting thoughts and emotions. The square-jawed he-man crushed her in a powerful embrace. "My darling, I'll never let you go," he swore.

Her knees were weak. The hot-blooded Spaniard had broken through all her defenses. He was all she'd ever dreamed of.

The sound of distant gunfire shattered the silence. Only yesterday, she would have been scared out of her skin. But she had come to see that life was cheap in this banana republic. In the back of her mind, Melinda knew she would never be at home here, but she would stay by the side of this Latin lover who had stolen her heart.

Clichés become clichés for a reason. At some point in time, every cliché was a fresh or surprising turn of phrase, and it expressed something so well that it entered the language as a unit of meaning, in many cases operating like a single word. Often, one of these boilerplate phrases is perfectly acceptable. To say that somebody is "drop-dead gorgeous" conveys an idea without distracting attention from the general thrust of the narrative.

There is a critical point, however, at which the constant use of off-the-shelf phrases saps the life from your writing. Because they are so familiar, these phrases are drained of even the meaning of the individual words that make them up. We skip over the phrase "pretty as a picture" without picturing anything; at best, it means no more than the word "pretty" alone, and at worst, nothing at all.

Clichés and common expressions also offer the potential danger of being too close to the thing to which they refer. They can create a momentary, or even permanent, confusion in the reader's mind as to whether he should take something literally or metaphorically. If your character has a gimlet eye, we recommend that she drink something other than a gimlet.

The explorer knew that his trek would be filled with pitfalls.

On the day of the marathon, Joe got out of bed and hit the ground running.

Finally, because of the lowest-common-denominator selection process by which clichés spread, they generally convey only the most ham-fisted ideas and are inappropriate for writing that requires precision or nuance. Clichéd expressions should particularly be avoided when trying to describe key emotions, important actions—anything the reader will want to experience in detail. Clichés paint with broad strokes and are best reserved for the familiar and unsurprising. If that describes the key emotions and important actions in your book—oops!

And in your heart of hearts, you know this is true.

I Mean This!! It's Important!!!

Wherein the author punctuates hysterically

Men were *so* difficult! At first Jack seemed to be so *into her*, but now Melinda didn't know WHAT to think! He'd seemed *so cold* when she ran into him in the alley the other night, surrounded by his work associates, who were all **such rough men**!!!

Perhaps she was doing the Wrong Thing, she thought as she headed towards their rendezvous by the abandoned wharves. How did she know he wasn't up to *something—something*—UNCOUTH?! It was getting dark, and the doorways were all full of Loose Women in their paint and *cheap* scent. She HATED that type, the type of woman who sold her most Precious Asset that was meant to be **sacred** to her husband!

Suddenly! she spotted Jack, and **her heart melted**— like a heart that had been frozen, but then was subjected to heat. "JACK! It's ME! I'm *so glad to see you*!" she said, and ran to him, **All Her Doubts Forgotten**.

The exclamation mark is the most commonly abused form of punctuation. While commas, often appear, randomly in unpublished manuscripts—and there is an epidemic—of unnecessary—em-dashes, it is the exclamation mark which takes the most punishment.

We understand that you are excited to be a novelist, but there are very few occasions when you should use an exclamation mark, and all of them are in dialogue. Even here they should be used sparingly, usually to indicate that a character is in fact shouting. Here is an appropriate use of the exclamation mark:

The last thing he expected when the elevator door opened was the snarling tiger that leapt at him.

"Ahhhhh!"

Overuse of exclamation marks makes them dwindle in significance until finally they carry no more urgency than a period—but one that graphically pokes you in the eye as you reach the end of each sentence. They are even more of a liability while they remain functional, and the reader responds to every one. Then the writing appears to be engaged in frantic hand-waving, straining every muscle to convince the reader that the action is important. Where the action is not important, this will seem bizarre and random, like underlining the word "the." Where the action is important, the exclamation points are like so many speed bumps: they pause your story to focus attention on the punctuation.

In almost all situations that do not involve immediate physical danger or great surprise, you should think twice before using an exclamation mark. If you have thought twice and the exclamation mark is still there, think about it three times, or however many times it takes until you delete it.

Other typographical conventions used for emphasis—italics, all caps, and bold—should likewise be used *infrequently*, VERY RARELY, and **never**.

Similarly, some writers, displaying either an admirable knowledge of sixteenth-century English literature or a fondness for the German way of doing things, will Capitalize Important Nouns, or Anything Else that seems Significant. (This is not a reference to those writers participating in the current vogue for self-conscious Ironic Capitalization; we are speaking here to those writers who assume that Love and Honor deserve initial capitals because they are Eternally Important.)

There are specific ways in which initial caps are used in contemporary English; fortunately, these are explained in the many style guides available.

9

SENTENCES AND PARAGRAPHS

*Though it seemed as if Jason had ever been among the ones favored
if ever there was one, no.*

Writers find that they can get the most out of words and phrases
when they are arranged in sentences. And, as sentences are expo-
nentially more complex than words, your opportunities to go
wrong now increase at a breathtaking rate. Every one of the
techniques listed below will get your manuscript a sentence of
Unpublishable.

The Minimalist

Wherein synopses take the place of writing

Mike hit him with a metal bar and the man fell, dead.
Mike left hurriedly, realizing he was going to have a
murder rap. Getting in his car, he drove away fast, heading for a hotel. At the hotel he sat and decided what to

> do. He called his girlfriend and told her to pack his things. The police found the body and identified the killer as Mike by fingerprints on the bar. Before the police could track them down, Mike and his girlfriend got on a plane to Europe. In Europe they went to the countryside and decided to buy a house with money the girlfriend had. "I need a gun, too," said Mike. They bought everything, food too. Then they settled down and lived under European names. That was the past.

Here, aiming for a terse, economical style, the writer delivers something that reads like a police report. This is the inevitable result of writing a page in the time it takes to cook a soft-boiled egg.

For a novel to work, it needs enough detail to bring the story to life in the reader's mind. In real life, the physical world effortlessly exists and is visible without anyone's help. In fiction, unless you describe it, it's not there.

That doesn't mean that every article of clothing and insignificant action should be described in full. Every novel slips back and forth between summary and scene. But you must do more than present an outline of significant events, with a few sound bites from important conversations. Those significant events and important conversations should be played out for the reader in real time, against a vividly described backdrop.

Writers of bare-bones prose often defend their work by saying they themselves are bored by reading description. These writers tend to be unaware of how important descriptions have been to the novels they have enjoyed. When well executed, description is unobtrusive and lends substance to a novel. It is the body fat of prose: too much is unhealthy, but without any, you no longer have the thing—you have its skeleton.

The List of Ingredients

Wherein lists substitute for description

The living room contained a sofa, an armchair, and a television set with built-in DVD player on a purpose-built stand. It had two windows, with curtains that were open. It was carpeted.

The zoo contained cages with animals in them. People walked past the cages, looking at the animals and talking. There were also places to buy snacks. The snacks available included hot dogs, hamburgers, and potato chips.

There were naked actors standing around the pornography studio: three women and one man. Two other actors were having sex on a bed. There were some cameramen filming them, who had their clothes on. There was a desk in the corner with papers on it, and a bulletin board with messages.

Sometimes an author understands in principle that description is necessary but does not grasp the difference between description and inventory. Characters having sex are given the same weight and emphasis as the bed upon which they are having it.

These same authors tend to focus on the generic items that are nearly always present in the setting described, rather than noticing the few things that make the living room a particular living room belonging to a specific person—the well-thumbed spelunking magazine, the bloodied mace peeping out from under the couch. We can assume that the reader knows that the cages in zoos contain animals. But give us the mangy tiger pacing in endless frantic circles around the fake log, and the zookeeper cursing in Ukrainian as the monkey steals his cigar—and it's no longer just any zoo.

The Redundant Tautology

Wherein the author repeats himself

An old man nowadays, with gray hair and wrinkles, Captain Smothers walked down the street to his weekly card game. Usually he would meet Katz on the way, and sure enough, coming down the street towards him he saw his old friend, Major Katz, who was as old as he was. It was the usual day they always arranged to meet for a game of chit with retired Rear Admiral Chortles. The three men, all former members of the armed forces, played chit, the card game known as "Priest's Delight" in Ireland, every Sunday. It was something they had never failed to do since they began the tradition. Katz joined Smothers and greeted him. "Hello," he welcomed Smothers.

"Hello," Smothers greeted him in return. The aged, decrepit, grandfatherly Katz was wearing a clean shirt and freshly ironed pants with shoes. He looked neat as usual. Smothers' shirt, however, was wrinkled and needed ironing; he had never been as neat as Katz, but rather untidy, though he too, like Katz, was formerly in the Army, but no longer. You would have expected an Army man to develop the habit of neatness, but Smothers somehow never had, and remained quite sloppy. They turned into the cafe where Chortles was waiting, sitting in a chair with his upright military posture, his back perfectly straight and erect. The two new arrivals sat, each in a chair, and the waitress, knowing their order from the many years they had been coming, brought the usual three mugs of beer to the three old military friends Smothers, Katz, and Chortles.

If you have made a point in one way, resist the temptation to reinforce it by making it again. Do not reexpress it in more flowery terms, and do not have the character reaffirm it in dialogue ("Spruce as ever, Katz!"). This point is worth repeating: don't reiterate.

If you have given your hero a curious scar in the shape of a lightning bolt on page 1, it is reasonable to mention it again later, by way of reminding the reader. To mention it again later in the same paragraph, however, is not aiding the reader's memory but trying his patience. (Of course, this does not apply to passages primarily *about* the characteristic.)

Another version of this is the "large gray elephant," or the "rectangular room with a floor, walls, and ceiling." While it is not absolutely a shooting offense to characterize an elephant with attributes that all elephants possess, it is a yawning offense. "An aroused and angry elephant" gives us a specific and striking mental picture. "A large gray elephant" gives us two extra words.

The Legal Brief

In which the language of officialdom predominates

Since they had first interacted, the two had experienced an increasing attachment with an ability to express feelings that mounted steadily. The initial emotional cold-ness she had perceived in Jack was increasingly vitiated by moments of greater intimacy in which he displayed a capacity for jollity which contained a portion of tender-ness. Melinda's role in this developing closeness was cru-cial: it had proved essential that she disregard her nega-tive assumptions about members of the male gender and privilege the negative capacity which is commonly called "trust."

Finally the day came when Jack expressed his desire to attach himself to Melinda by conjugal bonds. This pro-posal of marriage was not an unexpected development, and Melinda had already resolved on a positive answer. She was less enthusiastic about his insistence that the honeymoon precede the nuptials, though the preference he expressed for a ceremony in his native Cote d'Eau more than explained the above-mentioned reversal of the usual order. "Okay," she told him as he led her down the dock to his boat, "I have empathy for your needs, and after all, we have already had intercourse on multiple occasions."

"Melinda, you make me increasingly certain you are the optimum choice for my life partner," Jack said passion-ately.

Legalese, officialese, and psychobabble are an increasing blight on amateur fiction. Having spent long years writing business letters, filling in application forms, and suing neighbors, the fledgling writer sits down to write a love scene, and out comes something that reads like a translation from the Vulcan. The language of the psychiatric assessment is mixed with that of the tax form in a heady brew of four-syllable words meaning "nice." The author's long struggle to master the stilted, deracinated language of officialdom has left him believing that writing must be flat and lifeless to be smart.

Especially indigestible is the version in which said language is employed with an intrepid disregard for its actual meaning (see "The Crepuscular Handbag," page 103).

Mouth-Watering World-Class Prose

Wherein the author writes in a manner more appropriate to an advertisement

World-famous toggler and man about town Linus Walping entered his spacious, well-appointed apartment and walked to the handcrafted artisanal windows, where he basked in the breathtaking and unparalleled vistas of the magnificent Lavish River awaiting his gaze. Just returned from a first-class whirlwind vacation with his girlfriend, the glamorous model/actress Rain Weste, at the luxurious playground of the upper crust, the deluxe five-star Splendidide Hotel and Spa in the heart of metropolitan Darien's top-notch nightlife and luxury shopping, Reginald looked forward to a delicious, mouth-watering repast, sure to rival his wildest dream.

Advertising copywriters are faced with a very different task than you, the novelist. They generally have only a few lines to get their message across—only seconds of the reader's attention—and they have for this reason developed a concentrated and artificial form of language, very different from what we generally think of as writing. Were a novel an aged and nuanced wine, advertising copy would be artificial grape-flavor concentrate: it is only by convention that we call it grape, and more than a little bit of the straight stuff can make you sick.

Flap copy, the description on the outside of a book, is often more like advertising than it is like writing, and it belongs only on the outside of books, where it can do its job of catching the attention of passing strangers. Finding it on the inside of books can make the reader respond as he would to any commercial, and change the channel.

TM™

Beginning in the late seventies and early eighties, writers like Stephen King and Ann Beattie developed writing styles that were often referred to as Kmart Realism. Throwing aside a general tendency in American fiction to treat brand names as superficial, transient detail that would work against the timeless, transcendent qualities of literature, the Kmart Realists found that referring to Sears furniture and Riunite wine was an effective method of summoning up contemporary American culture. However, writers following in their wake have sometimes misunderstood this, and filled their novels with indiscriminate shopping lists. Applying brand names can be a powerful way of conveying information—when it conveys information ("He had the kitchen torn out and completely refitted with restaurant-quality Subzero appliances, which he never used"), but not if it conveys nothing more than the generic would ("She put the bread in the General Electric toaster oven").

Hello, I Must Be Going

Wherein time in the novel is poorly handled

Dinner was served in the penthouse's dining room overlooking the Bay of Eau that sparkled below. The two unimaginably wealthy criminals were regaled with beveled grouse, *farsi* with rich corpuscles, and *peau de homme-blanc* in a light *bete-noire* sauce, followed by spumoni.

"This food is delicious," said the man known only as "The Dinner Guest," polishing off the several-course meal and dessert ravenously and wiping his mouth. "But the business I came to talk to you about—"

"Sshh!" the pitiless trafficker in human lives, Jacques "The Hyena" Derrida, hushed him, putting his finger to his lips. "Let's go somewhere else for this conversation."

They sat down on a park bench. "Ah, Cote d'Eau is lovely this time of year. But not as lovely as the girl whose heart you stole in a certain American 'night spot,'" the Dinner Guest sneered while he lit his cigarette.

The Hyena finally managed to say, shocked, "How did you know?" as he savored his fine Belgian cigar.

The Dinner Guest finished his cigarette and stamped it out. "Mon friar," he said in faulty French, and told him about his complex network of surveillance operatives before informing Jacques that he would let him off under certain conditions.

It is difficult to make time in a novel flow at a realistic pace, but many authors disregard the simple mechanical factors that would keep the action within the realm of physical possibility. It is all too common for a character to throw a ball against a wall, deliver a monologue about tax reform, watch a plane's progress across the sky, and then catch the ball, with no apparent surprise at this warp in the fabric of time. Teleportation is also a common problem, with characters shown departing Boston by car, then delivering the next line of dialogue from Cleveland, with nothing offered to account for the gap.

If you use a "while" or "as" phrase, be sure that the things that are happening simultaneously *could* happen simultaneously. This not only refers to heroes who shout defiance at the villain while hanging from a rope by their teeth, but also to those less glaring instances where timescales of simultaneous actions conspicuously don't match up. *As his hair grew out again, finally brushing his shoulders, Joe applied humectant.*

Time in a novel, however, is not exactly like time in real life. In a novel, important events are depicted in real time, or even in slow motion, while events that are not a crucial part of the narrative are given cursory treatment. A long dinner takes a few words; a brief scene of violence may take many long paragraphs. Often the only reference to dinner (or the tennis game, or the drive to New Orleans) that is necessary is the word "after": *After dinner, they sat in the hotel lobby to discuss the new field of ergo-draulics. Soon the discussion became heated . . .* leads into a scene in which Nefaro is wrestled to the ground and made to eat hair—which of course will be rendered in all its gruesome detail.

The Penis-like Sausage

In which metaphors are inappropriate

Her nose perched on her face like a seagull, arching its wings to create two well-defined nostrils. The mouth below was thin as if actually consisting of only one dimension, like the loops which are the fundamental building blocks of all matter in string theory. Her eyes were blue as a flower. Brown from the sun, her skin was unblemished and pure like a paint sample of Crown brand's "Sandstorm." Her stomach was as flat as the Earth was once believed to be. She moved as lightly as a mote of dust gamboling in a sunbeam passing through the stained glass window of a French Gothic cathedral. Her breasts stood up proudly like twin tin soldiers. Looking at her made him feel an uncontrollable urge to vomit forth his innermost feelings, straight at her. He looked away at the sky, which had broken out in the blotched acne of sunset.

A metaphor or simile should be accurate in the comparison it makes, and appropriate to the mood and context in which it is used. It might be true on some scale that a girl is as beautiful as the Chrysler Building, but because the types of beauty are so disparate, the reader will be stopped short without a conversion table. Likewise, it is no good arguing that blood *does* leap out of a cut throat exactly the way juice squirts out of a juice box when a toddler falls on it; though the description may be physically accurate, it distracts from the drama you are attempting to convey.

Another common problem is the ant-carrying-a-cheese-puff metaphor, where the metaphor dwarfs the thing it is meant to describe. This results when the metaphor requires so much explanation and context that by the time the reader has fully composed the mental picture, she has completely forgotten the thing it is meant to illuminate. Metaphors involving complex concepts, like those that refer to quantum physics, Church history, or algebra, will usually stop readers dead in their tracks;

they are best reserved for novels that are actually about the world
of quantum physics, Church history, or algebra.

Linearity Shrugged

*In which the author assembles
the novel in no particular order*

Melinda would never have guessed that she would find
true love in the arms of the ruthless terrorist to whom
she had been sold like a hardware fixture by the man she
had trusted with all her most intimate papers and docu-
mentation. The beans were still too hot to eat. In the
early 1900s, Tripoli had been a small market town, where
goats could be seen not only in the streets, but making
themselves at home on the Persian rugs in fashionable
homes. So much had changed, and Melinda wished she
could have seen it in the old days, just as she often felt
about her hometown in Massachusetts, whose popula-
tion had quadrupled since the tech boom. "Comfortable,
my sweet honey of the rock?" Al al-Haig whispered, slid-
ing the bottle of third-date wine over the sand to her.

Marxism was only a thin veneer over an ancient trib-
alism in these parts. Later that day, in the Congress of
Herdsmen, the firebrand Al-bin Albino raised a color-
less fist to expostulate, "Allah condemns the ways of the
infidel! Long live the just and holy government of our
leader!" The air was dry and scented with the exotic krill
and catamite sold in the souk. Since the revolutionary
years, the political system had stabilized into fiefdoms
which were loyal to the Fief and his Fezzes, after which
the colorful local headgear had been named. The popular

tango band, Fife and the Fezzes, was unrelated, often causing Melinda a private smile. Made of finest batskin, the tassels were prized throughout the Orient.

Just as the elements of a plot must seem to flow logically from one to another, the sentences that convey your ideas must lead smoothly from one to the next. For those occasions when you want to change the immediate subject, nature has given us the paragraph break.

This does not mean that if you begin your paragraph with "The beans were still hot" you must keep on message with "heat of beans" until the end of the paragraph. You could move by easy stages from the meal itself to the emotional context of the meal; you could discuss the differences between Libyan and American dinner etiquette.

But the paragraph break alone cannot do all the work. If each paragraph in your chapter refers to a different topic, the reader will soon give up trying to make the connections. The larger ideas contained in paragraphs should lead from one to the next as well.

Every time you move from topic to topic, the transition should proceed by a logical association of ideas.

Gibberish for Art's Sake

Wherein indecipherable lyricism baffles the reader

Childhood had been squalls from the dried well of a primal force contained within the tender membrane of his infant yearning. He looked at the photo again, the delicate features of the child melding into his electric memories in bat-like gyrations of scarlet-hued mind. Beauty was lost in the pain that guided him back. Ever back, to the chthonic quagmire of yesterdays that ate yesterdays in monarchic succession, like crocodiles held vassal to a Pharoah of loss. Sweeping himself up in a pile, he discarded the good—always the good—in favor of agonizing meta-knowledge that was only about, never of! It was the "of" that could save him, or a pitchy unknowingnessness that eluded his feeble scrabble upon the tenebrous shale, granite, and basalt moon-surface of origins, submerged like tubeworms clustered about a primal vent, waving in the deep ocean currents, their angry futile colors seen only by fish born blind.

Some writers are convinced that since great modern authors like Joyce and Faulkner are difficult to understand, writing that is difficult to understand is therefore great writing. This is a form of magical thinking, analogous to the belief that the warrior who dons the pelt of a lion thereby acquires its strength and cunning. Using words like "plangent," or metaphors that compare the protagonist's suffering to a set of rosary beads baked into a cake that goes uneaten, does not of itself make your writing art.

We will at this point remind you that the purpose of writing is communication.

There is no substitute for saying something, and the reader should be able to discover what it is you are saying without having to call and ask you in person. While we understand that you are looking forward to the moment when an editor calls to ask what your novel means, and is so taken with your brilliance that he offers you a seven-book contract on the spot—we checked, and this is never going to happen. If the average reader cannot make sense of what you're saying, it is not a badge of honor; it is a badge of solipsism, and it's a safe bet your writing just doesn't make sense. Revise for clarity, even if it means betraying your natural lyrical gift.

Also, in case we weren't completely clear, the lion-pelt thing doesn't work either, so don't get any ideas.

The Unruly Zit

When the author has read too much Bukowski

His thinning puce hair allowed a flaking, unevenly reddened scalp to peek through; the greasy strands clung obscenely to the diseased skin, whose protruding moles and pimples, combined with a brownish sheen, gave the appearance of unhealthy liver tissue. On the wall behind him were tacked up pages torn from the crassest pornographic magazines. Over the years they had become saturated with grease and blotched with the smeared bodies of cockroaches. As he spoke, a noxious odor escaped through his dark yellow teeth, making Missy cringe, feeling an acrid taste of pre-vomit in the gluey membranes of her throat. It was a stench which seemed to emanate from deep in his bowels, perhaps the effect of years of constipation, which had given his every utterance a whiff of roiling, impacted excrement. "That's a dollar, even," he said.

"Thanks," said Missy, "but could I get that with extra cheese sauce?"

There is a certain category of authors whose characters are ever farting with abandon and sneezing meatily, and whose personal hygiene is described in terms of microbiology. Every scene takes place against a backdrop of rotting garbage feasted upon by coughing rats, by blankets of cockroaches, and by the protagonist. Especially jarring is when the hero and love interest seem to belong in a Victorian medical museum.

While gross details have their place, they should not be relentless. Readers will generally find such descriptions repulsive. They will go on to find your characters repulsive, your book repulsive, and harbor strong suspicions about you. This is not the progression most likely to end in a generous book advance.

Confine your gross-out scenes to those points at which readers ought to experience dismay. If the horrifying torture in the dank basement is repellent, all well and good. If everything is repellent, the reader will depart for healthier climes.

A final note: despite what you learned in junior high school, gross things are not, in and of themselves, funny. The jokes you laughed at again and again in Farrelly Brothers movies work only in conjunction with actual comic material.

Ya Hadda Be There

Wherein the author thinks you know what he means

Joe felt so different now. It was a completely overwhelming feeling that he couldn't pin down. He sat down on the cliff edge and scanned the vista below. It was perfect. Everything was perfect. The mountains against the sky were like nothing he'd ever seen before, and the air was just the right temperature.

He thought about the week he had had, discovering that his true father was Barrington Hewcott, richest—and swellest!—man in the world. He sighed, blown away. It was so cool. Just thinking about it made him feel incredible. Barrington was such a great guy. It was the things he said, but even more, the things he did. Maybe the things he had. Or maybe it was just the way he was.

Of course it was also good that Barrington was so generous. Some of the things he'd given Joe were priceless. From now on, Joe would be living in a really great place. Maybe now he would find the kind of girl he really wanted. A really cool girl who was just his type.

He got to his feet to walk back, but not before taking a last look back at the scenery, which totally defied description. Life could be so intense sometimes!

It is fine to show the world of your novel refracted through the reactions of your characters—but we still want to see the world, not just those reactions. The reactions themselves must be vividly described if they are to mean anything to the reader. "Amazing" and "terrific" are not descriptions, nor are "awful" and "horrible." Saying that something "defies description" conveys nothing but the author's defeat.

It is not enough that your character finds an Andrew Lloyd Webber musical "gut-wrenchingly awful." We must know how it differs from other musicals, or other Andrew Lloyd Webber musicals, that might also have been "gut-wrenchingly awful." What was it about the show that made this impression on your character? Was it the somersaulting cats, the roller-skaters pretending to be a choo-choo train? All these details will add up to give your reader a sense of the wracking, inexpressible awfulness of the experience far more clearly than the word "awful." While value words like these can be used in description, they should never be used to replace description.

10

DIALOGUE

"Meanwhile, Judy shook her winsome locks," the interesting man from Michigan expostulated.

"But I cannot understand why we are all talking like robots who have previously been discussed," Judy rejoined, startlingly.

In dialogue, your reader comes into unmediated contact with your characters; the author, by convention, is quoting them directly. If their voices sound real, they come to life.

Therefore, you should avoid at all costs writing dialogue that sounds like something an actual person might say. This is not as simple as it seems; no matter how hard you try, something recognizably human often slips through. We have therefore gathered the best techniques for making your dialogue unspeakable.

Asseverated the Man

When the author thinks he's too good for the word "said"

"It was a dark and stormy night," he divulged. "And, far

from the coast, we had no fear of any sea creature. How wrong we would be proved!" he appended.

She queried, "It was a sea creature? How is that possible?" she further wished to determine.

"It was a sea creature," he affirmed, "but one which had subtly mutated to be far more dangerous, far more deadly, than its marine counterpart. For on dry land," he uttered, "it had become both larger and more muscular. It's funny," he smirked, "now that I look back from safety."

"Funny?" she interrogated.

"Hilarious!" he expostulated.

"Surely not?" she doubted.

"But how little you know!" he exclaimed.

"Says you!" she objected.

"That's the last I am willing to say," he concluded. "Some listener you turned out to be!" he snorted.

Published authors use the word "said" almost exclusively when they wish to indicate that a particular character is saying something. "Said" is a convention so firmly established that readers for the most part do not even see it. This helps to make the dialogue realistic by keeping its superstructure invisible.

Many unpublished authors, however, become uncomfortable with the repetition of the word "said" and try to improve the technology of dialogue by substituting any verb that has ever been associated with speech or language.

A particularly egregious version of this occurs when an author conflates a stage direction with the desire to avoid the word "said" and instead of writing *"You and what army," he said, thrusting out his jaw* or *he asked, quirking a brow*, produces something like *"Hello," he thrusted* or *"Are you going to finish that?" he quirked*.

The only thing any of this does, though, is draw attention to the unconventional verb, which reminds the reader that there is an author, who is struggling mightily to avoid the word "said."

There are of course exceptions: "asked" is used for questions, "shouted" is used for a character who is doing so, and there will occasionally be a good reason to use a word other than "said" for plain speech. But spicing things up with "importuned," "vociferated," or "clamored" will sabotage any attempt to make conversation sound real.

Said the Fascinating Man

Where the author tells you
what you think of his dialogue

"It broke in through the window, bringing with it a characteristic fishy odor," said the gifted raconteur. "Soon we were all pressed up against the wall, trying to save ourselves," he added terrifyingly.

"What was it? A burglar with really bad breath?" asked the hilarious boy.

"No," said the stranger with a mesmerizing facility with words. "It was not."

"Was it a fish?" the girl said eloquently.

"No! No fish, this!" the man said poetically.

Do not try to manipulate the reader into finding a character's dialogue fascinating, amazing, frightening, or humorous by announcing that it has these qualities. If the dialogue isn't fascinating, claiming that it is will annoy the reader. Even when the quality asserted really exists, pointing it out undermines the effect.

Said the Man Who Had Just Returned from Three Months on an Arctic Expedition

Where the author misplaces his exposition

"All that was left was a scene of devastation," said the foreign man who had narrowly escaped being eaten by the creature that was holding Cincinnati in a grip of terror.

"Was your sister dead?" asked the terrified bookish child, who had always been afraid of the sea, and never more than now.

The slim, dexterous, craggy-faced dog food distributor retorted, "That might have been better, after what had been done to her! Ah, the peaceful forgetfulness of death," he said in a voice that recalled the sweet trusting face of his younger sister, and the horrible cries he had heard on that August night after which his baby sister, named Eglantine at birth, but always called Eggy, had been a mere shadow of her former boisterous self.

"What is your name, anyway?" asked the inquisitive child, whose name was Bruno.

"Oh. Name's Fred," said the usually reticent, but currently rather more garrulous than usual, Fred.

Speech tags are one of the places where long tracts of explanation do not go. Most speech tags should consist of two words: "[NAME]" and "said." Not "The burly [NAME] said." Not "The tall, many-freckled [NAME], who had been rendered timid and anhedonic by her relentlessly critical mother, said."

Just: "[NAME] said."

Substituting the pronouns "he," "she," or "it" works equally well.

In almost all circumstances, the only information that can comfortably be appended to a speech tag is a simple and concurrent action, such as " . . . [NAME] said, as he slathered mayonnaise on his burrito." That is, actions or thoughts that are occurring while the character speaks, or directly before or after, can be tacked on.

Action can even in some cases replace the speech tag by indicating the speaker.

"It was the size of a house!" Fred quickly downed his whiskey sour.

Or

"There was nothing I could do! It was yellow . . . yellow and green!" Fred turned away from the sisters, hiding his shame.

Information any more complex or distant, however, feels out of place.

"Fuck You!" He Said Profanely

Where the author uses adverbs to no purpose

"I don't know what you're talking about," he said, baffled.

"You don't see the connection? That's amazing!" said Harriet incredulously.

"Well, whatever it is that's killing the cattle, that's tragic, of course," he said with sadness. "But what it has to do with—"

"Tragic? Is that all you have to say?" she said, angry at his lack of further things to say. "That's the kind of thing that makes me doubt your intelligence," she said dubiously.

"Perhaps I know more than I'm letting on," Fred said mysteriously. "Anyway, you can go. I'm not here to be insulted," he added dismissively.

"I'm happy to go," she said ironically. "I'll take my
theories to someone who'll listen!"

Some beginning writers weigh down their speech tags with
adverbs that tell the reader what the character is feeling, although
it is patently obvious from what she just said. Other writers have
been taught that there should never be adverbs in speech tags
at all, under any circumstances; that adverbs in speech tags are
inherently wrong.

We feel there is a middle course. It is only when adverbs get
into the wrong hands that things get ugly. Adverbs don't kill dialogue; careless writers kill dialogue.

Overuse at best is needless clutter; at worst, it creates the
impression that the characters are overacting, emoting like silent
film stars. Still, an adverb can be exactly what a sentence needs.
They can add important intonation to dialogue, or subtly convey
information. *"I love you, all right?" he said jokingly* is miles away
from *"I love you, all right?" he said coldly.* But avoid at all costs *"I love
you, all right?" he said lovingly.*

"Ironically," We Said, Ironically

*Ironically, the one day we had set aside to write about irony
was the day we had to do our ironing before our blind date.*

*Ironically, our date turned out to be the one person in
the world we were hoping to avoid.*

*Ironically, our date turned out to be the one person in
the world we were hoping to meet.*

Ironically, we blinded our date.

Ironically, our blind date saw right through our pretenses.

Irony as a word and a concept has been so thoroughly stretched and abused by writers published and unpublished that it is now virtually meaningless, routinely applied to any situation in which one thing bears some relation to another thing.

Try it . . . it's fun!

Ironically, the pope actually was *Catholic.*

Ironically, the bear passed up all the other pastries and chose the bearclaw.

"Ironically" can often be replaced with "Wow," or "Dude, check this out!" with no change in meaning.

We would tell you how it should be used, but in a book called *How Not to Write a Novel*, that would be too ironic. (Feel free to check any of the standard references; we recommend Fowler.) We will tell you this: There is never a need to tell your reader that something is ironic. *Ironically, it was the very cat he had impregnated in the first place!* If it is ironic, the reader will notice. If it isn't, asserting that it is ironic will not make it so.

Sock Puppetry

When all characters speak in the voice of the surrounding prose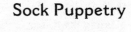

At last the crack team of child detectives had solved the dastardly crime. Little suspecting the trap that had been laid for them by the diabolically cunning dowager known as *le* Lady Leigh, the plucky kids broke into the factory and discovered the stores of prionate extract waiting to be added clandestinely to the beef by-product.

"These stores of prionate extract are destined for the homes of millions of innocent American boys and girls," Bruno explained to his intrepid friends.

"Should we not act to prevent it, children all over the heartland, from Maine to California, will, sometime between two and thirty years from now, display increased thresholds of irritability," the cheerful Topsy put in.

"More terrifying still is the prospect of an entire generation going about their lives unaware that they might have turned out in a slightly different manner," said Pip, the grump.

"Setting to work quickly, we will avoid detection," Bruno advised.

They were busily stowing packets of dried calamari in their rucksacks when the bodyguard, Moe, appeared, straight from his hardscrabble immigrant life in Hell's Kitchen.

"Desist from your work," the bodyguard warned. "I am training a gun on your childish heads."

Many authors neglect to give their characters a voice which is distinct from the narrator's. This results in a seventy-year-old classics professor, a down-on-his-luck boxer out of Memphis, and a high-class hooker all using the same turns of phrase. Often, they're all speaking in exactly the same inappropriately formal and stilted voice, presumably meant to be literary.

Some writers are apparently working from a submerged idea that all writing should sound loftier than speech. Some simply find it difficult to pin down what it is that makes dialogue sound natural. One way to accomplish this is by using contractions, which are often curiously absent from unpublished novels. Many beginning authors seem to believe that contractions, like sexual intercourse, began in 1963, and nobody before that year ever said "I'm" or "don't." Others believe that contractions aren't used by anyone with a graduate degree, a country-club membership, or a British passport. Still others would seem to be unaware that contractions exist.

Happily, conversation is all around us, research for the taking, and wrong notes in manuscript dialogue can often be spotted by reading aloud and listening to yourself. While dialogue is not exactly like speech in real life, it will work only when it creates the impression of actual conversation. Otherwise, it sounds like conversation in an unpublished novel.

The Convention of the Invisible Men

Where the author fails to identify his speakers

"But surely that's genetically impossible?"

"That's just the crazy thing about it. Because the germ works on a germic level, once it gets into the DNA, nothing is impossible to the resulting mutation."

"But—humans giving birth to—?"

"That's not all. Have any of you ever asked yourself what would happen if a germ could work its way up to the brain and survive there for years, controlling the host's behavior down to the very clothes it chooses to wear, and the show tunes it hums?"

"My God. Did he say Germans?"

"No, germs!"

"That's the stuff of nightmares!"

"Exactly."

"How long do we have before . . ."

"Shhh. I can't hear him."

"I don't know why we're listening to this."

"But surely that isn't what happened—?"

"No."

"Yes."

"And furthermore, the children will continue to give birth to—"

"But why is he doing that thing with his fingers?"

"If you don't stop talking, I'm going to call an usher."

If speech tags are not the place to reveal a character's childhood traumas or the ups and downs of his career in law enforcement, and if they're not a place to demonstrate all the different words that can be used to indicate speech, what are they for?

They're there to tell you who's talking. Without speech tags, the reader soon loses track of who's saying what.

Some authors insist on omitting speech tags because they feel their characters' voices are so well written and distinct that the reader couldn't possibly confuse one for another. After a few back-and-forths, though, it's far too easy to lose track of who said what last. If the absence of speech tags goes on for more than a page, your reader is almost guaranteed to have to stop and count backward to the last identified speaker, causing him to think, "If only the author had used speech tags, I wouldn't now be wondering why he didn't use them."

Also remember to toss the reader an occasional reminder of where the conversation is taking place, and what is going on around it. Bare naked dialogue will eventually plunge the reader into a nightmarish science fiction scenario in which two brains are conversing telepathically while suspended in a lightless tank of nutrient-rich fluid.

(If you are in fact writing a novel about two brains conversing telepathically while suspended in a lightless tank of nutrient-rich fluid, carry on.)

The Court Reporter

In which every single last solitary word of conversation is included

"Hi, Harriet," said Jane, sitting down at the restaurant table. "Sorry I'm late."

"Hi, Jane. Nice to see you," said Harriet.

"Have you been waiting long?" Jane said anxiously.

"No, don't worry. Only five minutes."

"Oh, that's not bad." Jane smiled, relieved.

"No, I was late, too. The buses were a nightmare."

"Yes, the trains were no good, either. Yikes."

The two laughed. Then Jane picked up her menu. "Have you decided?"

"Hm, the *shrimp boulevard* looks good." Jane frowned in concentration. "Or the *squash tournament* . . . is that vegetarian? I guess I can ask."

"Jane, I'm beginning to be afraid that compounds present in the creatures' brains may cause their strange behavior. Using them as a protein source may have deadly consequences . . ."

Just then the waitress appeared to take their order. "Hi. Would you like to hear the specials?" she said perkily.

"My god, surely this can't mean—"

"I'm afraid so. The author is actually going to list all the specials!"

Some authors, in an attempt to mirror reality, clutter their dialogue with all the polite chit-chat and workaday detail that occurs in real life. This is one of those instances when reality must be put aside in the interests of realism, as well as to avoid having your readers tear their hair out from the relentless, unbearable boredom.

"But I want to represent life in all its mundane, stultifying detail!" you might protest, "And that's how real people speak." True, but those very same people will not sit still to read it. As a novelist you are always selecting what to leave out and what to put in, and just as you don't mention it every time your hero blinks, you should generally leave out the information-thin social niceties. For similar reasons, while real conversation is liberally peppered with filler words like "um" and "well," dialogue should use them sparingly.

An appropriate gambit for the above would be *Arriving at the restaurant five minutes late, Jane made her excuses as she took her seat in the booth. Harriet was looking harried. "About the results of the autopsy,"* she began.

Don't Mind Us

When the author forgets that other characters are present

The meeting began with a few prefatory remarks by the Mayor. As luck would have it, Jane and Alan found themselves seated next to each other at the far end of the conference table. Jane studiously avoided looking his way.

Alan took out his pen and began tapping it on the table, something he knew got on Jane's nerves.

Jane glared at him. Alan smirked. She darted her hand out and snatched the pen from him.

Alan glared back, but his look soon softened.

"Jane . . ."

"I don't want to hear it."

"Jane, don't you know how sorry I am?"

"You should have thought of that before you and your cousin—"

"Second cousin, okay?" Alan interrupted, his tender feelings forgotten. "It's not illegal."

"What*ever*!" she said. "If she was two months younger, it would be."

"If you were a little more enthusiastic in bed, instead of bringing up your so-called trauma every time I touch you, maybe you could complain," Alan said, bitter. "I get it, okay? Seeing what your father did to Fluffy was horrible. Well, that was twenty years ago. Time to get over it."

Jane shook her head, angry. "That's what I get for trusting a neo-Nazi!"

"Of course! Blame my politics!" Alan pounded the table with his fist, nostrils flaring. "You and your Jew friends would just love patriots like me—"

"Shut up, Alan! Shut up!" Jane shrieked wildly, grabbing his collar and shaking him.

When the meeting was over, they filed out with their colleagues, comparing notes on the Carb-Free Detroit! campaign that the Mayor had detailed.

Fictional characters, when they need to share with one another confidences about grisly crimes, deviant sexual antics, or plots to overthrow the government, often seem oblivious to the fact that they are sitting in a car with three strangers. The strangers themselves, apparently morbidly polite, say nothing.

This is because the author has forgotten they are there. Focused on the plot unfolding within the dialogue and the characters who are at center stage, the author overlooks the scene he has described before the conversation starts, which included people. While you can mention the potted plant in the corner without altering the scene, if you stand a person there, you have to remember that your scene has an audience.

Likewise, most people know not to talk to themselves in public, and if they do, it will usually elicit an odd look or comment. In Unpublished Novelville, however, the streets would seem to be filled with characters walking along deep in earnest conversation with themselves, and no one bats an eyelash when a man in a crowded bus cries out, *"Now I see it! I must kill Monique to save us all!"*

Remember the context. If you must have your characters plan the bombing of the Pentagon in a packed elevator, at least let them do it in a whisper.

Doublespeak

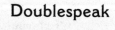

Where the author inadvertently makes characters seem dishonest

"You know I'm entirely on your side, Alan," Harriet said. "The welfare of Americans comes first with me."

"Thank God I can trust you," Alan said, wiping sweat from his forehead with relief. "I was really beginning to feel alone."

"Of course you can trust me," Harriet said sweetly. "You can relax now. Just leave it in my hands. And how is your nice girlfriend doing? Still hearing wedding bells?"

"Couldn't be better," said Alan, looking down. "She's a sweet girl. Sure, everything's just fine."

This scene is absolutely okay—as long as both characters are lying through their teeth. If Harriet *is* on Alan's side, and Alan and his girlfriend *are* getting along just fine—the scene is unintentionally misleading.

It is surprisingly easy to unwittingly make a character sound dishonest. It often happens because dialogue is too straightforward and unequivocal. Any character who says *"I would never lie to you"* is understood to be lying. Likewise, if a character repeats the same point over and over—*"Sure, I can defuse one of these. Your cat will be perfectly safe. I can do this with my eyes closed."*—by the third repetition, we assume that he is about to be proven wrong.

Stage directions can also unintentionally indicate dishonesty. If you mention an incidental action at the wrong moment, it can be taken as a significant comment on the dialogue. Those which show that a character is nervous, or which seem to conflict with the emotion that the dialogue is meant to express, are read as signposts of dishonesty. *"Of course I'd tell you if something had happened to Fluffy,"* *he said, fidgeting with the napkin* tells the reader that Fluffy is no more.

"Hello! I Am the Mommy!"

Where characters announce things they wouldn't

"I love my work. Some people call me a workaholic. Well, maybe I am," said Annette, gathering her files. "I believe that work is the most important thing in life. That's what makes me a successful account executive."

"As your sister, I think I understand you better than most people," said Nina, nodding understandingly. "We have the same hot temper and the same commitment to what we believe in."

"Yes, but I'm the smarter of the two," Annette clarified. "I can understand complex ideas easily, and I have a keen problem-solving ability."

"Whereas I am the more intuitive one, with an empathetic and open nature rare in a tall, blonde, attractive, accountant of Scandinavian descent."

Sometimes, in an effort to convey information about a character, an author will ascribe to the character dialogue that sounds like a five-year-old playing Barbies.

In real life, the only situations in which you hear people describe themselves in this sort of straightforward manner are when they are introducing themselves on a television game show, or when you are on a first date with a narcissistic bore.

Especially bizarre is when a character named Desdemona, apparently discomfited by the extravagant name the author has chosen, explains on page 1: "I know my name is unusual for a girl from rural Michigan. It was given to me by my mother, who was an English teacher and revered the works of Shakespeare. I think it suits my romantic and ethereal nature."

Most bizarre of all is when she is speaking to her husband. We call this

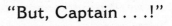

"But, Captain . . .!"

*Where characters tell each other
things they both already know*

"The fact is, our Cincinnati, Ohio, apartment is adequate for two bachelors, but I feel you should get your own place, now that you are engaged to your blonde girlfriend, Jane, who virtually lives here, as I've told you many times before."

"Yes, and I agreed, but I will miss you. We've had great times together, like the time when you dressed up as a woman and pretended to be a strip-o-gram at my birthday party. I played dumb all the way, just to see how far you would take it. Well, we both know how that ended! You got naked and made a clumsy attempt to tackle me, as you recall." Alan chuckled ruefully.

"Yes, and though that became a source of distance between us when I came out of the closet early last year, considering that you are as straight as a straight arrow, we've now moved past that to forge a deeper bond, where things are understood without having to be put into words."

Characters in unpublished novels often spend page after page happily telling each other things that both of them have known for years. Nothing is taken for granted: a character is reminded of how he came by his nickname; colleagues recap how they came to work together; spouses remind each other of their marital status. While in real life, people do, irritatingly, tell you things you already know, they do not generally go so far as to explain "I am wearing a green shirt, while you are dressed in your favorite white dress."

Because it is so obvious that this is the author addressing the reader, it creates an impression similar to a television actor turning to address his lines to the camera instead of looking at his fellow actors.

"And That's When the Vaginal Thrush Returned . . ."

When characters inappropriately share intimate information

She sat down at the counter and ordered a cup of coffee. The waiter was a handsome, fiery man of about her age, and they naturally fell into conversation.

"What's wrong?" he said. "You have a wounded look in your eyes that makes me think you're going through some painful issues."

"Yes, my husband has been cold to me for years, so I've decided to make a break with him and start fresh," she said. "It's so painful to be betrayed by someone you love; it's like when I first found out my parents weren't actually my parents. It shatters your heart."

"Oh, women like you who leave their marriages because they don't feel 'loved' are what's ruining America," he opined. "You must be a really selfish person."

"You clearly don't know anything about relationships. I have to be patient with you, because you feel threatened by what I have to say."

"You probably think I want to sleep with you. Well,

think again," he said, pouring her a refill. "All the women love me, but I'm pretty choosy about where I spend the night."

"You would sleep with me if I wanted you to," she said. "In fact, why don't you come to my hotel later?"

"Okay," he decided. "Though once I've shown you what a real man is like, you'll probably fall in love with me and turn into a sick, obsessed stalker."

Okay, your new character knows nothing about your protagonist, and you've set up a situation in which they would legitimately be having a conversation. So full steam ahead with the backstory, right?

Wrong again.

While some people value strangers because each one is a potential friend, we've always liked them because that's one more person whose life story and innermost thoughts we won't have to hear. People sitting next to us on the crosstown bus are very unlikely to tell us about their unhappy childhood, the ongoing tragedy of their mother's alcoholism, or their foot diseases. If they try, we change seats.

Even close friends express certain thoughts and opinions only with great care and diplomacy. A relationship requires a good deal of history before it can survive a simple factual statement like "You smell bad."

Likewise, while an opinion like "I am above average in my sexual performance" is held by many, if not all, it is generally openly declared only in jest.

Also, while the purpose of the author is to show us the character's inner nature, it is very seldom the purpose of a character. The character is nominally a person, and people wear a public face that is different from what is going on inside. While some people will share their latest therapeutic breakthrough with strangers at the drop of a hat, it is because they are universally shunned, and strangers are the only ones they have to talk to. Unless you intend your character to be a pariah, she must be shown to shed the normal inhibitions and defenses before she shares her deepest self with her new friend/love/stranger-trapped-in-an-elevator-with-her-with-no-hope-of-survival.

For similar reasons, characters should not make sudden about-faces in their attitudes. They should not, for instance, immediately capitulate when the protagonist "proves" that their worldview is idiotic. Though we may occasionally recognize that we are wrong, or regret a stance we have taken ("I don't care about the money; I write for the love of the novelistic art!") the need to save face dictates that time must pass, and a circuitous route of rationalization be traversed, before we admit to having changed our tune.

El Foreigner

Where nonnative English speakers are rendered poorly

"Señor, es surprising that mad squid disease, she jump the species barrier so easy," said Pedro, the janitor, who was studying systems biology at night school. "I am astonished. You are contento, that I am staying here while you review los samples?"

"Sí," said Alan, politely using his few words of Spanish.

Pedro blushed. "Meester," he said, "You are all right, or as we say in my country, homosexuales."

"Bok choy!" cried Fred Cho, evil mastermind of the

mad squid outbreak, as he burst into the room, waving his .38 Wabash. "Kimchi bok bok!" Spluttering with rage at the scuppering of his bio-plot, he had lapsed into imprecations in his mother tongue.

Pedro pointed a finger at him angrily. "Hijo de puta! Hold the tongue!"

It is difficult to render foreign English without falling into unintentional comedy. Some errors, however, can easily be avoided.

Do not have a foreigner address everyone as "Señor" or "Monsieur" despite speaking otherwise perfect English. Do not sprinkle the conversation of a Mexican with the few Spanish words you have picked up along the way. These are generally the same words that the Mexican would have learned in English *first*, like the words for "yes" and "hello."

It is also generally a bad idea to try to render foreign accents phonetically. An Italian saying "He's-a gotta pretty-a daughter-a" may offend some people, but it will convince no one.

When doing any kind of accent, whether regional dialect, foreign accent, or a characteristic like a lisp, it is important to remember that a little goes a long way. Under no circumstances should you attempt to render the speech as it actually sounds, so that it looks like this:

"Ah doan know wha yawl lairn yaw chillin laik that."

No matter how good an ear you have, and how perfectly you've captured it, it soon becomes a task to read. The reader is forced to sound out each word, like somebody studying ESL, and will soon grow impatient. Instead, one or two well-placed words sprinkled throughout are enough to flavor the whole thing.

A particularly problematic version of this is when writers

attempt to render the speech of the illiterate or ignorant through misspellings, like this:

"Heez ded? I sed it ud kill 'um."

Remember: stupid people are no more or less phonetic than anyone else. Since the character is speaking, not writing, any errors in spelling reflect upon the writer, not the character.

PART IV

_____

STYLE—PERSPECTIVE AND VOICE

What's the point of you?

Most novels you see on the shelves of bookstores and supermarkets are written in the third person, with POV (point of view) staying close to that of the main character, so that we learn things as he does and are privy to his emotional turmoil as the story unfolds. (*With a chill of fear, he set Fluffy free; now there was no turning back.*) Some novels may avail themselves of several points of view; typically, the author shifts perspective at the beginning of a new scene.

For a greater sense of immediacy, many successful authors choose a first-person narrative (*I raced as fast as I could down the stairs, away from the innocent-seeming cat*) or tell their story in the present tense (*I shift uncomfortably beneath the tarp. The ticking sound grows louder. Has the cat found me?*). In all these cases, authors use interior monologue to enrich the story, which is mainly told through action.

You, the unpublished novelist, know that all these authors lack vision. You are free of the petty conventions that would bind you to the intelligible. No small-minded editor polices your work, insisting on "cohesion."

So, if your character stops for gas, why not just jump straight into the head of the gas-station attendant while he fills the tank? Back on the road and nothing much happening? Don't worry! People don't think about only important stuff. Is that a rattle your character hears in the back of his truck? He can think about that for 10,000 words, easy. Did he hear a sound? Or is that the sound the truck always made, and he never noticed? It's a kind of a rattling sound. There it is again—a sound!

Hey, this is the stuff people actually think about! And since publication isn't an issue, you have all the room in the world for this meticulous realism.

But why stop there? Aren't you kind of curious to know what's wrong with the truck? Well, who knows better than anyone else? The truck! Let's hear what the truck thinks about its owner, its gas mileage, and that cute Volkswagen that's been pacing it since Ohio. And, in a final stroke of genius, jump back to your character's POV, thinking, "It's like my truck's taken a shine to that little car there. It's amazing how machines can seem almost human."

This is just one of an infinite number of ways you can use POV to avoid publication. With just a little imagination, the possibilities are literally endless (What was the Volkswagen thinking? How must the gas feel, knowing it must inevitably combust? And is that a hitchhiker we see up ahead? Bet he's still wrestling with childhood traumas—let's find out!).

This is only the beginning. Below, we have rounded up the most popular ways to turn a simple boy-meets-girl story into convoluted and wearying unintelligibility.

11

NARRATIVE STANCE

"Am I the third person?" I wondered.

The novice unpublished novelist chips away at the prospect of publication one element at a time. The truly masterful unpublished novelist, though, has the vision to safeguard his amateur standing with one broad stroke: choosing a narrative perspective that is completely wrong for his story.

I Complete Me

Wherein the novel is a work of auto-hagiography

He could still hardly grasp it. He, James Slappingham, the man who had given so many women their first orgasm—women who told him that he was the only one who knew how to "do me just right, baby"—that it could happen to him!

He was only fifty now, and looked closer to forty.

That waitress today, when he'd asked her as she was taking his order, she'd guessed his age at thirty-five. Sure, most of his hair was gone, but he knew women instinctively responded to that as a sign of virility, rather than aging.

And the extra forty pounds—it seemed to make women more comfortable with the lust he inspired in them. Twenty years ago, coeds in the park were so confused and overwhelmed by their feelings that they had to walk away, some of them obviously angry with themselves for what they were denying themselves. Now they seemed much less disturbed, more like all those young waitresses he always won over with his sexiness. In fact, he was certain it wouldn't be long before one of them would go out with him.

And then, he knew, just like the many hookers he'd introduced to their true orgasmic ability, they would be grateful.

That had been the plan. But the evidence was too plain; it had happened too many times to deny it any longer. I was impotent.

Autobiographical fiction is perfectly acceptable, and a priceless resource for writers. Many authors make entire careers out of recycling their experiences, or even out of recycling the same experience many times. But the recurrent theme of their books is not "There is more to me than people think" or "They'll be sorry when I show them all." In fact, successful autobiographical fiction tends to go the other way, using themes like "I am a loathsome worm" or "I flounder helplessly with the simplest of tasks."

While the "I" that suddenly erupts in a third-person narrative is the easiest way to look foolish when writing self-aggrandizing autobiographical fiction, it is usually superfluous; if this "I" were the only giveaway, it would be a copyediting issue. Instead, it is generally the tip of a massive iceberg of self-revelation.

There Is No "I" in Book Deal

Symptoms of the Auto-Hagiographical Novel

- scenes in which the protagonist realizes that everyone underestimates you, or, um, him
- scenes in which the protagonist is victimized unjustly by versions of your family members, colleagues, or friends.
- scenes in which versions of your family members, colleagues, or friends have a change of heart and beg for forgiveness
- departed lovers who realize their mistake, to their great regret when they find they are too late
- scenes in which a middle-aged protagonist is pursued by besotted teens
- long passages of exposition obsessively parsing the protagonist's qualities
- long passages of exposition explaining that the protagonist, though a weak link in her insurance firm, is secretly a literary genius
- a plot line in which a work of literary genius penned by the protagonist is published to earth-shattering acclaim

None of this means that you cannot write a novel in which, say, a Victorian chambermaid, after being unappreciated by her family members and the kitchen staff, charms the handsome Duke de Hazzard with the brilliance that shines forth in her verse. And everyone likes a fantasy, so there's nothing wrong with a novel that showcases the sexual prowess, nerves of steel, and devastating charm of a James Bond–like secret agent.

But fiction that hews too closely to the specifics of the author often lacks the alchemy that transforms a personal wish-fulfillment fantasy into escapism satisfying to others.

Grabbing the Mike

Wherein the point of view momentarily strays

Nunavit sighed as she saw the ragged band of her fellow Eskimos returning exhausted from another failed walrusing expedition. Winter was closing in, and she didn't know what they would do for food if this bad luck continued. It was the work of the foreign priests, she was certain. They had destroyed the people's faith in the animistic gods whose worship had sustained them through millennia in this unforgiving climate. The white man's God had brought them guns, liquor, and Cuban cigars, yes. But without the walrus meat to provide a protein-rich diet, none of them would live to enjoy those city pleasures.

Aquavit trudged up to her, dragging his great harpoon. Her heart ached at the sight of his weary, emaciated face. Until now, he had always been the cheerful one, the jokester who smiled through thick and thin. Now he was glowering, hungry, and disgusted by his fellow hunters, hunting itself, and all the hundred kinds of snow. All he wanted to do was trade this damn harpoon for some liquor and a Cuban cigar.

"Never mind," she reassured him as they rubbed noses. "When I fetch the talisman of the ancestors from the forbidden place, the walri will return; I feel certain of it!"

Sometimes an author slips into a different point of view for the space of a single paragraph, or even a sentence. This is especially jarring when the entire remaining novel is given from the point of view of a single character, whom we have come to regard as our second self. It gives the feeling of a fleeting and unexplained moment of telepathy, an uncomfortable intrusion of somebody else's thoughts. When the protagonist's point of view resumes, we move forward in the narrative warily, ready at any moment for a fresh assault on our minds.

Point-of-view shifts can even consist of a single word. For instance, the point-of-view character, an actor who has been thinking smugly about the reviews of his recent film, is suddenly referred to as "conceited." Clearly, the author wanted to convey this opinion of the actor, but the actor himself would not be thinking this, so we are suddenly yanked out of his head and scrambling to understand who we are now. The same disturbing effect can be achieved with speech tags like "He boasted" or "I sniveled."

Generally, any point of view that lasts for less than a page should be cut. And if you have chosen a restricted third-person point of view to start with, you must accept the restrictions that come with that choice.

The Tennis Match

Wherein the point of view bounces back and forth

"But who's going to pick up the pieces after you go?" Ann said angrily. She glared into his face, trying to find any trace of the sensitive man she had fallen in love with years before. Did he even remember that she had needs?

"Oh, it's all my fault," Joe said. "Like you had nothing to do with it." His voice trembled. Although he was trying to put a brave face on it, Ann looked more beautiful than ever. How could he leave?

Ann sat on the edge of the bed and burst into sobs. It was all so hopeless! He would never understand!

Joe watched her cry, feeling the usual desperation. Why couldn't he ever please her? Sometimes he thought that was all he needed: to see her happy.

Ann wished, how she wished, he would just hold her.

Should he hold her? Joe wondered.

Hold me! Ann thought. There's still time.

Was it too late? Joe thought.

Go on, Ann thought.

No, Joe decided, shaking his head, it's too late. I will try that new scruffing lotion, and then it's splitsville for yours truly.

So, you wrote Chapter One from Ann's point of view as she throws Joe's shirts out into the street. Then you wrote Chapter Two from Joe's point of view as he shops for skin care products. Now they're together in a room. Surely you can use both points of view, because you set that all up—right?

No. Even if the reader has been previously introduced into

Joe's *and* Ann's minds, she has no wish to jump frantically back and forth from one to the other. Regardless of the setup, this alienates the reader from both perspectives. She is unable to identify with either because there's no telling when it will be yanked away.

Avoiding Ann's point of view through a scene, even though we've been in her head before, is a preferable technique. The reader feels confident that sooner or later, she'll get to see what Ann made of it all. For the time being, the reader is left in suspense, which makes her do the only thing that meets everybody's needs—Joe's, Ann's, and yours—turn the page.

Persona Non Grata

Certain late twentieth-century novelists used the second person singular successfully—notably Italo Calvino in *If on a Winter's Night a Traveler* and Jay McInerney in *Bright Lights, Big City*. But there it ended. There was no consequent rush to adopt this gripping technique. No new genre was born; established authors were not forced to reexamine their use of first person singular. In fact, it was named the "second person" when McInerney became the second person to get away with it and it became clear that he would also be the last. The reason is that all this innovation had to offer was what any innovation has to offer. It was new.

The key word in the previous sentence is "was." It *was* new, and newness is perhaps the least sustainable of all qualities.

When first confronted with a second-person narrative,

the reader thinks "Oh, this is one of those second-person things." This is the only point at which your daring departure from convention makes an impact on the reader.

From then on, "you" functions exactly like "he" or "I." The reader is not persuaded that the story is actually happening to *her*. In fact, the reader quickly becomes desensitized to the buttonholing tone of *you do this, you do that*. The editor, though, does not have time to become desensitized between thinking "Oh, this is one of those second-person things" and chuckling to himself as he thinks "You are now rejecting this novel."

Very occasionally, an editor sees past the contrivance and buys such a book—on the condition that the author revise it completely into a traditional third-person narrative.

The Democracy

Where everyone is heard from

Having lost his faith after the spaying incident, Reverend White had left his congregation and become a drifter. Now he stood in yet another seedy, low-life bar, nursing his tequila and musing on the many twisting paths he had walked. How dark was the road that led from Minneola to this lawless Mexican *frijole!*

"*Hola*, handsome," a señorita accosted him. She sized up the powerfully built gringo. He would make a nice change from the usual dirty drifting drifters she slept with for a peseta and some *brouhaha*, the tasty local shrimp dish.

The hard-bitten barman watched the interchange with a private grimace. How many loveless pairings had passed through the *puertas* of his *cowabunga!*

"*Hola,*" White said, but inwardly he shrank, reminded of his wife. Wistfully, he bent down to scratch the head of Fído. Fído's tongue hung out, and he wriggled with pleasure. The señorita smiled, for the furry *amigo* was the closest thing she had to a friend.

The mariachis struck up another jaunty *polka,* their faces solemn as they mused, each on his own private sorrow. If only he could earn an extra *tortuga* tonight, thought mariachi player #1, then he would finally have one more than mariachi players #2 and #3. Ah, how he would gloat, then!

So many bootless lives floated, turning in the dusty winds that criss-crossed the lonesome plains of the *piso mojado!*

So you're using an "omniscient" narrator. You have given yourself the freedom to know the history of all the world, see into every mind, and explain the chemical formula for dishwashing liquid in a scene where the only animate character is a backward child. So now you're ready to write the party scene from *everyone's* point of view at once! What amazing insights that will give the reader into the complex social dynamics of the Waxman bar mitzvah! It will be the Rashomon of bar mitzvah novels.

The only problem is that by the time you've gone into Waxman #3, all the reader is doing is trying to keep track of who the point of view character is. When every POV in the room is given equal time, you no longer have a novel; you have a focus group.

In commercial fiction, if you wish to use an omniscient point of view, you must first create an authorial voice that belongs to the omniscient narrator, not to any (or all) of the characters. From this base, you can dip into people's thoughts at will, but for this to work, you must develop a deft control of point-of-view shifts. If you simply jump from head to head as the mood strikes you, the voice becomes a fractured mess.

Reading Over Your Shoulder

Wherein the characters
seem to hear each other's thoughts

Betty looked over at Joe, the man she wanted to spend her life with—but did he only want her for the life her multi-billion-dollar toggle empire could give him?

Joe scowled at her. "I love you, Betty, and not for your money. All I want is to make my own way in the world, like a man."

Joe was so sensitive! She didn't know how to assure him that it was his wit, his insight, his ability to fasten complex toggles, that had attracted her, from the first time they met at ToggleCon '06. Oh, the Winnipeg Hilton! The communion of thousands of toggle enthusiasts brought together in one place—a place where Joe could shine.

Joe sighed and turned away to the window. "Toggle-Con seems like such a distant dream now," he said. "In harsh reality, my fastening isn't enough to hold you."

When a character responds to another character's interior monologue as if it had been spoken aloud, the reader gets the impression that the characters are reading the book right along with her. This is a glaring lapse, a moment when the reader is forcibly reminded that none of it is real.

A related problem is when a point-of-view character somehow knows everything about other characters' histories, about what is going on in another town, or about civil engineering—because the author does. There must be an obvious or reasonable way for information to have reached a character. A character can of course have studied civil engineering, or heard gossip about somebody before they've met—but remember that this knowledge must be plausible *before* the knowledge is exhibited. It is no good having the ten-year-old child comment on a wine's "corkiness" and then hasten to explain, after the fact, that she was raised in a family of Mormon vintners.

Similarly

The Paradigm Shift

When the characters are of one mind

From his corner office on the top floor of the Edifice Building, Joseph Third IV looked out over the lesser office towers of Metropolis City. The founder and CEO of the most powerful hedge fund in the tri-state area, Third made other businessmen know the fear that only businessmen knew.

As he looked from his window, which jutted out over the city like the prow of a great ship, Third realized that he was like a pirate of yore, sailing freely in the seas of capitalism, owing fealty to no power but himself, raiding lesser ships captained by lesser men. He could almost feel the wind lifting his hair as he glided over the waves—

"Boss," his assistant, Pulpy Credlar, said from the door. "Your four o'clock is on his way up."

"Send him in, Pulpy. He's in for the fight of his life."

"Yes, sir," Pulpy said, miming a sabre thrust in the air. "We'll make that lubber walk the plank together."

Sometimes a particular character will have an insight that creates a new framing metaphor for the story—which is then inexplicably adopted by everyone else in the novel. Of course, this is because the insight is actually the author's, and having informed the reader, the author then feels free to proceed as if the idea is "common knowledge," shared by all.

Where this misstep doesn't bring the reader to an exasperated halt, it can create the impression that two characters have been conversing telepathically, or passing notes behind our back. When it involves all the characters in the novel, it can give the reader a momentary sensation of dislocation, a stutter in reality, as if he'd somehow blinked and missed the chapter where everyone discussed the similarity of a hedge fund to a pirate ship. In either case, the reader quickly recovers, but the novel does not.

The Service Interruption

Wherein the point of view suffers a temporary blackout

I thought of Fafnir's lovely face, chalky with fear as she was dragged away by the drones. There must be a way to reprogram those soulless cyborgs. I was sweating as I tried to think. Everything hung in the balance. At last

I turned to Jake and told him my plan. "This is what we'll do . . ."

Birds sang in the trees and the sun was beginning to show through the clouds as I spoke. There was a tang of spring in the air.

"That's brilliant!" said Jake, when I was done. "They'll never suspect a thing. But have you solved the riddle that's baffled us ever since it was posed by Colonel Frown's robot henchmen?"

"Of course!" As I told him the answer, a light rain began to fall. The trees trembled in the wet breeze, exuding an arboreal aroma.

"Magisterial!" said Jake, when he had understood. "A diabolically clever solution. I want to see Frown's expression when you spring that on him."

"That will have to wait." We jumped into the cyber-Porsche and sped off to the dramatic confrontation that awaited us.

Here the writer craftily conceals what the point-of-view character is up to, to maintain suspense. But since we have been comfortably settled into that character's head for some time, to be unceremoniously booted out feels completely unnatural. Excluding important information once the scene is under way gives the reader the frustrating sense of reading a censored document, where intrusive black blots cover all the stuff he most wants to see.

A straightforward solution is to not write scenes where characters say things you don't want the reader to hear, or where point-of-view characters mull over things you don't want the reader to know.

Life on the Margins: POVs to Avoid

The Innocent Bystander

Where possible, point-of-view characters should not be there to do the work of a security camera. Mayfly point-of-view characters who briefly get a voice because they witness an event the author wants to show can sometimes work, particularly in narratives that already have numerous points of view. In novels that are otherwise confined to the perspective of one or two main characters, it is jarring and can do more harm than good.

The Genyuss

Writers who try to write from the point of view of a character who is smarter than they are should consider asking that character if this is a good idea before proceeding. It is therefore usually a bad idea to write from the point of view of God. Likewise, writing from the point of view of an enlightened yogi or mystic usually comes out sounding like the point of view of a psychic hotline.

King Lear from the Point of View of the Throne

Writing from the point of view of a spoon, the world's smartest mosquito, or Nero's fiddle is generally inadvisable. The author is immediately faced with the task of accounting for the spoon's ability to type, interest in human affairs, etc. (Unless it is a literary novel, where such things pass without comment.) Writing such a book is very difficult, and such strained gimmicks generally backfire. So unless you have an inner passion that drives you, willy-nilly, to sing the secret life of the toaster, it's better to look to the toaster's owner for your protagonist.

Tenses: The Past Oblivious

Wherein the verb tense shifts unpredictably

The doctors had said that only the most advanced medical science could diagnose her, and after months of mysterious symptoms that stumps all the regular doctors, Sally found the best-trained diagnostician in the upper Midwest, Dr. Fenton.

Being a devout Christian, when Sally learned that Dr. Fenton was a Christian Scientist, which meant he was not just a scientist, but a Christian as well, she knows that this was the doctor God meant for her to see.

Waiting in his reading room, Sally looked at the inspirational posters on the wall. Yes, this was a place of hope, she told herself. She hanged in there, just like that kitten is.

The door opens and Dr. Fenton, a man of heroic faith in a profession filled with the faithless, called her into his office.

"The tests are back, Sally. I'm afraid the results aren't good. You have advanced ovine stiffening."

Sally was shocked and says, "AOS? What will happen to me?"

"Without the simple shot that would clear it all up, the stiffening will continue until you suffered complete ovine failure." He looked at her sadly and shakes his head. "How I wish I could help you."

"Oh, Dr. Fenton. If only it had been a treatable condition."

"They're all untreatable, Sally. Now pray with me. Pray with me, while you still can."

Often, in the heat of creative inspiration, the author finds herself slipping from one tense into another unawares. While walking across a room, a character time travels from present to past and back to the present again. A fire that was being lit is burning. Dogs bark as they trotted behind their master. The reader can usually decipher these time warps, but soon that is all he is doing. Rather than feeling suspense as the hero races to the scene of the accident and found the heroine barely alive, he's just glad it's over . . . if he can even be sure it isn't yet to come.

Always carefully revise your use of tense *before* submitting a manuscript.

Tenses: The Past Intolerable

Wherein a single tense is used for every event

I kept my secret all through law school, and nobody suspected a thing. I was hired by a top law firm, and was three years from making partner. I would shake the very timbers of the monolithic structure of American jurisprudence when I revealed what nobody suspected.

I remained true to my beliefs while I worked within the system, and I worked harder than anyone else to allay any suspicions that my hidden principles might arouse. I worked more billable hours than any other attorney at the firm. Ha! The fools! Soon they would all know, and then they would realize how thoroughly I undermined everything they believed about the system.

I shivered with anticipation behind my heavy oak desk, the door to my corner office shut just as the door to my true purpose was shut. On the day they made me part-

ner, I announced the truth for all to hear. That I, Archie
Teuthis, was . . . an *anarchist!*

English is a rich and nuanced language that has shaped itself to
meet the needs of its speakers. Just as English allows innumerable ways to say "You are making me tense," it provides us with
six different past tenses that allow the expression of any of the
many ways in which an action can take place in time.

These past tenses differentiate between actions that are ongoing and those that take place at a defined moment (*he was reading when she smacked him with the meat*); between actions that
occur before and after each other (*he had fully undressed before
he left the house*); and then further delineate actions that happened before *those* actions, whether ongoing or taking place at a
fixed moment. (*Having fully undressed, he was leaving the house
when she smacked him daintily with the meat. As he lay unconscious,
she thought: Has he been taking his meds? Indeed—had he?*)
And so on.

In spoken language, context often allows us to resolve any
ambiguity that might arise from so many possibilities. In fiction,
it falls upon the writer to differentiate between *he had been flensing* and *he flensed*.

Using the subtle machinery of English tense structure, you
can flash back a thousand years to deliver a fascinating piece of
background information, and then zip forward to the ongoing
scene without breaking a sweat. Neglect the subtleties of tense
structure, however, and your reader will be left behind in the
medieval epoch, straining to understand why the Carolingian
court are getting into a Honda.

12

INTERIOR MONOLOGUE

Darn it all! thought Pol Pot. Them snooty intellectuals get my goat bad.

If you've worked with us this far, you should by now have characters whose behavior is unbelievable, whose lives are unlikely, and whose interactions with others should get them quarantined. Make their inner lives equally insufferable by using any of these powerful approaches to bad interior monologue.

The Hothouse Plant

Wherein a character overreacts to every stimulus

"Could you get that?" he called. I trembled at his harsh tone, remembering times when he had only spoken to me in the timbre of love. The phone was blaring, shrieking, jangling my already raw nerves. As I picked up the receiver my voice was shaking.

"Hello?"

"Hello! I'm calling from A-1 Rug Cleaners and I have a very special offer—"

My heart was seized with bitter cold as I listened to the droning voice. The world had become so cruel, so impersonal. Where was the community? Where was the compassion? As I hung up on the telemarketer my eyes settled on a framed photo of my chihua-poo, Fído, who had mysteriously disappeared on a vacation in Cancun. Tears came to my eyes as I thought of poor Fído, cast adrift in this heartless world. May God keep you, I whispered in my heart as the tears coursed down my cheeks.

Sometimes an author replaces dramatic events with dramatic reactions to mundane events. Characters like these are always on the edge of tears, screaming fits, or hysterical laughter. Joy floods them as they find that mussels *are* on the menu. Despair grips them as they hear that the train is running late. They see a neighbor in the street—what an astonishing coincidence! All wounds are eternally fresh for such characters; ten years does not dull the pain of divorce, bereavement, or losing a watch.

Unless a character is teetering on the brink of insanity, his reactions to events should be proportional to those events.

Every Breath You Take

Wherein every passing mood is lovingly detailed

"I'm getting the *mussels verbiage*," he said, smiling at me in that way he had.

I smiled back, feeling a little wistful. "I think I'll get the *fracas medallions*," I said. I put down the menu, the wistfulness giving way to a gratitude for his presence.

He reached out and took my hand, sending a wave of love through me. "Still want to go to that hotel?" he asked.

I felt a slight tension, perhaps even anxiety. It had been so long since we spent the night together that I was afraid of what I might feel, when we were actually alone. "I want you," I said. "That's all I know."

As I said the words a deep relaxation swept through me. It was a mingled feeling of love, fear, despond, and salacious flusterment, with perhaps just a hint of restless leg syndrome.

It is not necessary to give us a play-by-play of your protagonist's every passing flicker of emotion. These emotions in themselves, furthermore, do not constitute action in a scene. They may be spurs to action in a scene, or reactions to events in a scene, but if they overwhelm the action, what you have is not a scene but an encounter session.

Failing the Turing Test

Wherein the character has no reactions whatsoever

But when he pulled the covers from the naked form, it was not his wife there at all—it was the lovely Veronica, his brightest and most eager graduate student, wearing nothing but a tattoo of Leonard Cohen.

"Hello, Veronica," said Professor Johnson. "What are you doing here?"

She pulled a gun out from under the pillow and sobbed. "I am here to kill you," she explained.

"Why?" he said. "I've never done anything to you."

She sat up, a beautiful vision in her youthful nudity and state of undress. The moon made her unblemished skin glow like something luminous, and her black hair fell over her slim shoulders like a cape of hair. She said, "You gave me a C!"

"I'd be willing to reconsider your grade if you'd do something for me," the professor said.

"Oh? What's that?" she asked, tossing the gun aside and thrusting forward her young breasts, her eyes dewy with willingness.

"I'll be needing a cat-sitter for two weeks in April for my trip to Cancun. Would you be available?"

While the emotional lives of characters should not be described in their every tiny wrinkle, characters must *have* emotional lives. When someone boos them off a stage, they should experience chagrin. When they fall from a tenth-story window, they should feel alarm. The writer should not count on dialogue like "Yikes!" to get the point across.

In fact, the author should "check in" with the point-of-view character's thoughts and feelings every so often, even when nothing dramatic is happening. If you don't, the character effectively stops having thoughts and emotions. And unless you are writing a zombie novel from the point of view of the zombie, you will lose credibility fast.

The way to do this is almost never to flatly report: *She felt chagrin. I was horrified. His feelings were hurt.* Generally, emotions should be shown indirectly, through some combination of thoughts, stage directions, and descriptions of physical sensations.

You'll Have to Go Through Me

*Wherein the fact that a character
has senses is paramount*

As I came into the room, I saw the light coming through the curtains and smelled the sweet aroma of the aspartame trees outside. I could feel the new warmth of spring in the air. I saw that Jim had taken his seat in the armchair, which I noticed was in need of cleaning. I could see deep patches of grease where his arms rested.

"Hi, how'd it go at Dr. Fenton's?" I heard Jim saying. Then I felt the hot tears begin to flow down my cheeks.

Sometimes the point-of-view character interposes herself between the reader and the scene, asserting repeatedly that she saw every object, heard every sound, and felt every feeling. Instead of "The pencil flew through the air, heading straight for my eye" we get "I saw the pencil flying . . ." Instead of "The ululations of the marsupials filled the night" we get "I heard the ululations of the marsupials fill the night."

This steps down the drama inherent in what's going on; it muffles the reader's experience. Unless the main point of a thing is the character's experience of it, give us instead the thing itself.

Hamlet at the Deli

*Wherein the character's thoughts
are transcribed to no purpose*

The gentle caterwaul of the frenulum moths mixed with the sweet piping of the frenulum moths, a background for the symphony of birdsong. One melody caught my ear, and I watched until I saw its author was a thrush.

Oh, how the thrush reminded me of my second wife! Why had I left her? I could only shake my head. I was a good and decent man, fully capable of loving another, of opening myself to another's love. I knew this from my experience with my first wife, whom I had loved fully and with all the tremulousness of youth. In fact, now that I thought about it, why had I left my first wife? Had I been callow? Had I been selfish? Maybe I wasn't a decent fellow after all. . . .

The manuscripts of unpublished authors are often rife with passages in which the protagonist takes stock of his life. Sometimes an entire scene is lovingly set up—looking out on a mountain landscape of surpassing beauty; standing alone at the end of a dock at sunset—for no other reason than to give the protagonist a romantic setting in which stock may be taken. Sometimes a scene even has a character doing things that facilitate stock-taking, as when the protagonist packs up his home, cleans out his closet, or looks through a photo album.

While an occasional reflection can be useful as a segue into a scene, or as a note within a scene, it should never itself be a scene. If your character needs to take stock of his personal issues, show him the respect he deserves by giving him his privacy.

Men of Inaction

It is not just characters taking stock of themselves that bogs down the work of beginning novelists. A very common characteristic of unpublished manuscripts is a wildly disproportionate ratio of inner contemplation to action. A two-block walk is occasion for twenty pages of inner monologue on how much you can tell about a person by his shoes. A glimpse of the ocean on a drive down US–1 calls up an entire chapter on the ecology of coral reefs and the lessons it can teach us about getting along with our fellow man.

The beginning novelist, being the sort of person who wants to write a novel, tends to come to the job with a backlog of thoughts and feelings, years and years of minute observations, exegeses of Conan novels, elaborate and detailed scenarios of how things should be. For years, the unpublished novelist has kept these things to himself, knowing from experience that friends and co-workers are much more interested in discussing things that happened, were about to happen, or who they happened to, and less what the novelist thinks about the contemporary decline in thinking.

And so, it all pours out, page after page, finally being expressed because nobody is wandering away to get another drink in the middle of a sentence. The unpublished novelist should remember that his potential readers are people just like the friends and co-workers who didn't want to hear this stuff in person. This is why published novels tend to begin with action, continue with action, and provide a steady supply of action, through which *relevant* inner monologue is gracefully threaded.

The Skipping Record

Wherein a character has the same thought repeatedly

"Well, young Huckleby, what have you to say for yourself?"

The shabbily dressed orphan searched his scattered memory to give the Archdeacon the answer that could change his life—and the life of his sister, Shabby Nell—forever.

The Archdeacon drummed his fingers upon his desk and arched a bushy eyebrow at the boy.

Nell had given up so much to help prepare Oliver for this audience—for if he only answered correctly, their destiny would henceforth be other than what it had heretofore been. It was so very important that he say the right thing!

"Harrumph," said the Archdeacon. He pulled out his heavy gold pocket watch and looked at it pointedly.

Oliver thought about how mightily different things might be in the future for he and his sister both, if he were accepted here for training at the Flensing Institute. After that, nothing would ever be the same.

"Now see here, young man, can you not tell me why you want to come train with us at the Flensing Institute?"

The tatterdemalion orphan shifted anxiously in his seat, knowing all that rested upon the next words that left his mouth, and not only for him! They would be pivotal in the circumstances of his sister, as well! Oh, if only he could remember!

Finally, fully aware of the import of the words he was about to utter, Oliver trusted himself to the guidance of his sister's fond ministrations and the goodness of the Lord, and spoke.

"Bum!" he said, and regretted it instantly, for every guttersnipe in Burbleby-on-Mire knew it was the thing one must never say to Archdeacon Flensing.

In real life, inner monologue is often repetitive. Having conceived the idea "She's hot," we will happily continue to embroider this theme in our minds throughout a twenty-minute conversation with a bored flight attendant. If you render these thought loops directly in your fiction, however, your character can begin to sound uncannily like a malfunctioning computer in a movie made before anyone had a computer.

Give us the thought once. We will assume that the character's opinion remains the same until you tell us otherwise.

Jekyll and Hyde

Wherein a character and his inner voice are mismatched

The china in the dining car rattled as the Orient Express sped around another mountain switchback on the way to Hong Kong. The assembled passengers waited for Remi D'Arnot, the finest detective in all Belgium, to speak. He had brought them here to reveal who had killed the Countess.

" . . . and so I zen contemplated who would have ze opportunity to commit this foul crime," D'Arnot said as he paced the aisle between the tables. "But could she be only ze crime of opportunity? *Non,* I say to myself, there is more to thees crime than meets ze eye."

He walked to the table where Professor Rasmussen sat with his shy niece. "It could not be ze Professor, for the Professor 'as"—he seized the professor's white gloves and yanked—"*no 'ands!*" The others gasped at the wooden prostheses now revealed.

D'Arnot walked to the table where Major Offal sat with his adjutant, Sergeant Nightsoil. "I pondered then the strange bee'avior of our military friends . . ." his voice trailed off as he suddenly realized that finding the monkey in the Major's trunks one half hour ago changed everything " . . . or per'aps *not* so strange. It might be too early to zay," the Belgian waffled.

Blow me! the diminutive detective thought. *Why do I do this every time? I'm such a freakin' idiot.*

If you are writing the character of a street thug, not only his dialogue but his interior monologue must remain in the vocabulary and diction of a street thug. This inner/outer mismatch appears under various guises. The character's intelligence may steeply drop or rise when she is alone with her thoughts; her social class may change; her gender may seem subtly, alarmingly, to switch. While there can—even *should*—be some distance between what's going on in someone's head and the face that person shows to the world, the reader should be able to detect some relationship between them.

A related problem is

I, Youngster

When the author is behind the times

Most people would be scared by the Black man at the door, but Ida wasn't most people. The lead singer of the punk music band, Disrespect Your Elders, Ida was used to people being scared of *her*. People would see her and wonder if she had a switchbladed knife. Pierced and tattooed, with spiky hair and badly made-up eyes, Ida was cool with a capital "C."

Because of Ida's fame as a punk band singer, people always noticed her, but tonight she was going to the midtown Marriott, the trendiest nightspot in town, and she'd taken extra care with her appearance. When she'd come back from the beauty parlor, Ida had put on her nicest slacks with daring go-go boots. She had decided not to wear a brassiere that night. She had a nice shape, and because of her bad attitude she wasn't going to hide it.

"Excuse me, ma'am, but your name isn't on the list," the Black man intoned, in a way that would intimidate most people.

"To Hell with your list, man," Ida said and met his eyes for a long moment. The Black man cracked first and looked away. Ida had won again. Hefting her pocketbook onto her shoulder, she walked past him into the Night Club.

If you are a mature person writing about a youngster of today, your own youth is certainly going to be one of your best resources. How did it feel to be so young and alive? What did the world look like at first encounter? Some things never change, and if you can capture those feelings, you're halfway to creating a believable young person of the early twenty-first century.

Some things do change, though, and if you don't learn which things, halfway is as far as you will ever get. When creating a character who is of the moment, you must find out how people sound now. Slang changes; styles change; attitudes toward sex, work, and bodies change. And the more of-the-moment contemporary detail is, the more fleeting it is likely to be: by 2005, the "World Wide Web" was beginning to sound like something Mr. Burns would say to Smithers. To write a character set in contemporary culture, you must be familiar with contemporary culture.

It's fine to use the idiom you're familiar with—in fact, we recommend it—but if you're not writing about a primitive cryogenics experiment gone awry, it might be best to set the novel in a period when that idiom was current.

Preemptive Strike

Wherein the author anticipates criticism

And so we found ourselves triumphant, all of the impediments to our love—once seemingly so formidable—overcome, alone together on our island home, swimming in bliss just as the dolphins swam below in the bay, joyful and serene. It was amazing how everything had turned out so perfectly—if I'd read it in a book, I wouldn't have believed it myself.

"You are my light in the darkness," Misty confessed, with tears in her blue eyes.

I smiled, thinking that it was hard to believe anyone would actually say something like that, and that somebody would actually take it seriously. It sounded just like a bad movie. But it was so different when it happened in real life!

Here the weary author, who can no longer deny the awfulness of what he has been writing, attempts to deflect criticism by acknowledging the glaring flaws in his novel. He will often go on to have the characters explain the problem away by pointing out that because it is real life, it is not subject to criticism . . . as it would be in a novel.

Of course, it is a novel, and nobody is fooled.

As in twelve-step programs, acknowledging the problem is only the first step. Readers will not accept your unbelievable coincidences or clichéd prose just because you acknowledge there's a problem. You must go on to fix the problem. A related issue is an author's attempt to maintain suspense by having the viewpoint character deny what is blatantly obvious:

Ha! I laughed to myself at the idea. My new boyfriend, a vampire? No way! Just because I never saw him during the day and his skin was pale and he went off on mysterious jaunts at night, coming back with a satisfied look on his face, and my friends, all the while, were disappearing one at a time . . . it was ridiculous! There were no such things as vampires in real life, so I was going to put that crazy idea right out of my head!

When the pay-off comes—he *is* a vampire!—no one is going to be surprised. If you want to hide something from the reader, you must hide it. It is not a help to have the protagonist repeatedly protest that it's not there.

Swann Song

Wherein a character ignores the scene that is occurring to reminisce about one that is not

As she walked into the swanky Manhattan party, Betty Jo felt a wave of boredom come over her. How she wished she were back at home with her family, strumming her banjo on the porch while Grampa Cornpone played the fiddle. Oh, the steamy bayou nights of her youth! Ma would cook up a huge pan of Creole innards, whilst Pa sat in the corner smoking his pipe of tabaccy with the hound dogs snoozing at his feet.

When the yodeling was done, she would sit dreaming for hours, gazing at the stars and swatting palmetto bugs and bats away from her face. The scent of the magnolia and home-cooked parsimony was lovelier to her than any fancy French perfume.

Two hours later, she left the party without having talked to any of those stuck-up Yankees. In the cab, she gave herself over more fully to dreams of home.

Having no interest in describing the setting in which she has placed her character, the author goes into a fantasy about something she finds more interesting.

She imagined this ballroom as it must once have been.

I gazed out the window and remembered the purity of the Arctic snows.

She imagined how it could have been if only Reynaldo were here.

It's perfectly all right for a character to go into a reverie about other times and places if the memory contains important information—and if the present scene does finally take place. If the memory or fantasy entirely supplants the present time, however, readers will wonder why you bothered to take us to a party in the first place if you weren't going to let us talk to anyone or dance.

PART V

———

THE WORLD OF THE BAD NOVEL

*It would be a long, hard battle, Jim knew, and he would be alone
for most of it, but someday, pants would be optional in Delaware!*

Just as characters have an inner and an outer life, so does the
world of your novel. The outer life is the setting—the physical
world in which the story takes place. Many authors use the world
of the novel and what happens in it to convey a message, too, an
underlying theme: the novel's inner life.

While the outer world of one bad novel shares much in
common with the worlds of other bad novels— buildings, trees,
cats—every unpublished author seems to have hit upon a message that is unique to them—and will stay that way, if there's a
God in heaven. The ranks of would-be novelists are filled with
Holocaust deniers, men who question whether women have
souls, followers of Ayn Rand. This is a priceless tool in avoiding
publication. The overall message of any bad novel should make
the staunchest First Amendment absolutist long for the Thought
Police.

In terms of technique, remember that the reader is incapable of drawing inferences: the message must be stated, in no uncertain terms, on every page. Long passages should explain how the scene just enacted is proof that "crime doesn't pay." Back at the precinct, Sergeant O'Reilly is saying to his partner, "Just goes to show you, Jack: crime doesn't pay." But perhaps the reader still isn't getting it. Perhaps the reader even *disagrees*. Add a scene in which a character who disagrees with your spokespuppet is ridiculed, humiliated, and finally crushed by a runaway elevator. Good work! You have ensured that the readers of *Shoplifters Roast in Hell, Too* will never read another word penned by its author.

But before you start broadcasting your message, you must attend to the setting: where and when your novel takes place, its social milieu, its bricks and mortar. The favored approach is to omit this entirely. Keep the reader guessing about where events are happening, what historical period the characters live in, and whether at any given moment they are jogging, taking a steam bath, or dangling from a precipice. Try to create an absolute nothingness in which, from time to time, a phone receiver or a pair of pert breasts materializes as the protagonist forms the intention to use them.

Is the novel a political thriller about American spies operating behind the Iron Curtain? Write a long first chapter in which a character named Randi eats chocolate and thinks about her weight problem. Is it a work of science fiction about a war with hyperintelligent cactus men from Planet Ouch? Lift your battle scene from one of Patton's campaigns, with the sole exception that the rifles and cannons gain the prefix "vap-," "plasma-," or "Feynman-." Ideally, the cactus men should swear in slightly antiquated English when injured, and description of them should be confined to the word "green." Even a tale of love and loss set in suburban Connecticut can baffle the reader who is never told that the tale of love and loss is set in suburban Connecticut, leaving him struggling in vain to picture settings called only "the house," "the restaurant," and "the town."

Now that you've butchered plots and annihilated characters, destroying entire regions and philosophies is a natural next step. Below we give basic strategies for making your fictional world uninhabitable.

13

SETTING

It was a town like any other.

The colorful people who swarm in the streets, the buildings that rear high over the odoriferous gutters, the very sky in its azure blueness—all are opportunities to baffle, alarm, and disgust your reader. Here's how to make the most of them.

The Sharper Image Catalog

Where tech-porn (shoe-porn, shelter-porn, etc.) halts the narrative

For the first time since he had received the assignment—hell, for the first time in his career as an international operative—James Gruff wondered if he was going to make it back to headquarters. He gunned the engine and burned rubber as he sped away, the gunmen of the Medellin cartel in hot pursuit. He would rely on his usual evasive maneuvers, but he knew that there were *Giardia*

Nacional stationed on every road between here and his only route out of the country.

Gruff sped on, shifting into third gear to gain a few miles on his pursuers. The car was a 2006 Montalban coupe, with double wishbone suspension both front and rear, and high-performance tires. The upholstery was the finest Corinthian leather, stitched in a herringbone pattern, with integrated headrests and power-adjustable lumbar support. As he drove he consulted the power-retractable mirrors, which had built-in heating to maintain visibility even in extreme weather conditions. He stamped on the gas, and the heel of his oxblood Ralph Lauren shoe dug into the floor mat, which was of the finest Shropshire wool . . .

Whether it is the getaway car, the murder weapon, or just the bed in which the two lovers consummate their furtive passion—it is presumably background. While it must be described, it should not be described in such exhaustive detail that it blots out any glimpse of the action.

The majority of writers will never have this problem. It is far more common to see *no* description, or a vague gesture toward description, than to see too much. But a certain minority get carried away with the minute details of the things the hero owns, the apartment he lives in, and the watch he uses to check the time.

Sometimes this is because the author, having discovered that he has a facility for writing description, tries to use description to convey everything in the plot. A love scene in a hotel room may consist of several pages on thread count, with a few lines of love talk stuck in the middle. Sometimes it is because the writer has a particular passion for the intricacies of gadgetry, weaponry, or designer clothes. Then the action is continually halted for passages that sound uncannily like product placement.

While a chick-lit novel should accommodate some drooling descriptions of quality footwear, and a techno-thriller would be little more than an overheated outline without the thrill of tech, a little goes a long way. And the right time for it is before action begins, or when the hero is patiently lying in ambush, not when he is racing for cover while he madly fires his target gray Ruger SP 101 .357 stainless steel revolver with removable side-plate, a heavy 25 ounces to reduce felt recoil, but compact enough to be concealed in the average pants pocket.

Current trends in entertainment have led to this increasingly popular version:

The Food Channel

In which the author stops to describe the specials

"They're famous for their seafood," Gruff said, narrowly regarding Pueblo Espadrille. If Espadrille even suspected that he was an undercover agent of the DEA, Gruff would never leave the restaurant alive.

The waiter came with their order, but as they were about to tuck in, they were interrupted by Espadrille's bodyguard, Estomago. With eyes narrowed at Gruff, Estomago leaned over and whispered in Espadrille's ear. A look of alarm came over Espadrille's face, immediately replaced by his signature icy cruelty as he stared at Gruff with a new awareness. With a gesture, he dismissed Estomago, his eyes never leaving Gruff's face. He said levelly, "So, Gruff, you are looking forward to your food? Let us eat together like civilized men a final meal."

Espadrille's *partridge famille* was served on a bed of *matelas de mousse*, with a *remulac* of vegetable saffron, and a sauce. Gruff had ordered the *dieux norse* a la carte, but he was also having a generous side dish of capers in aspic, garnished with *garniche*. They ate with relish, as well as with a *lapin-chocolat* chutney, savoring each bite. Gourmets both, they allowed the flavors to explode on their tongues, not hurrying the fine meal. They even stopped to exchange choice morsels.

Gruff knew he would have trouble finding room for dessert. Still, when the dessert cart came, he couldn't resist.

"I'll try the baked fritters," he said. Espadrille got the world-famous pecan log. Again, silence reigned as the men dug into the delicious treats.

While it should be clear that the rule of economy applies to dinner scenes just as it does everywhere else, beginning writers often feel compelled to give an account of the dinner orders of everyone at the table, and then to keep the reader apprised as to how good or bad the meal was.

It is true that in real life, people seem incapable of eating a meal without commenting on the relative goodness of the mashed potatoes, but this is one of the many points where novels cannot afford to be mimetic. If your characters are eating, the only interaction with food you should report is that which advances the plot or illustrates the mood.

If Pueblo's sherbet is treated with a slow-acting poison, we are happy to read a detailed account of him eating the sherbet. Likewise, if Gruff betrays his nervousness by fumbling his dumpling off the chopsticks, or follows a fumbled dumpling under the table, where he spots the device affixed to the underside of the table, please keep us informed.

Otherwise, food should be fast.

If your detective is a food critic, or the romance involves two chefs, the recipe should be adjusted accordingly, of course; but even then, don't stop the car chase because we're passing that marvelous little patisserie.

Magic-onomics

Wherein characters' funds issue from nowhere

Exiting her East Side duplex, Rain Weste paused for a moment and sighed. Another audition with no callback; it had been months since she'd even been offered a part. She would be feeling pretty depressed right now if she didn't know that shopping therapy was the medicine that cured all ills! Thank heavens she lived right next door to Barney's!

She spent the afternoon digging through racks of the most scrumptious clothes heaven had ever devised. From time to time she considered that she would have to go and register at that temp agency soon. Otherwise, how would she pay for her three weeks in Venice at the Palazzo Splendidorio? She also really needed new track lighting for her dining room. Not to mention that she had an appointment with Luis, Manicurist to the Stars. If only

she came from a rich family, like Binky, she would be able
to just relax and concentrate on her art!

In certain contexts, readers are willing to suspend their disbelief
to participate in a fantasy of luxury. No one worries about how
James Bond can afford those suits on a civil servant's salary. If
the credibility gap grows too large, though, readers will balk.
Characters who go on international excursions to follow the
mysterious woman who stole their heart need a source for their
astronomical travel expenses. Weekend aviators need an income
that would stretch to such an expensive hobby.

Half-baked attempts to justify a protagonist's mystery money
can also backfire. Explanations should amount to more than
"Somehow Rain had lots of money." Giving Rain an inheritance,
or explaining that she recently gave up her career at a top law
firm to pursue her art, will work only where these things feel
like part of the world of the novel. That is, the inheritance should
come from a plausible place and have a real history in the life
of the character. Ex-corporate lawyers should seem like people
who could have been hired by a law firm and succeeded at that
profession. This means, among other things, that they cannot
now be twenty-five.

Your character *can* win the lottery (find the bag of money,
inherit the castle) if your novel is *about* a character winning the
lottery, just as readers will accept an alien invasion if that is what
the book is about, but not if it is randomly introduced late in a
novel about agrarian reform (see "Why Your Job Is Harder Than
God's," page 28).

Character as Setting:
The Good, the Bad, and the Ugly

If you find you have written yourself into any of these worlds, it is time to start looking for the exits.

The Playboy Mansion
Some books are populated solely with beautiful people. This is all very well when the action is set in a modeling agency or in the Muslim paradise. If it's a police station, a high school, or just about any other setting, beauty should occur as often as it does in real life.

The Aftershave Commercial
A beautiful woman announces after a five-minute acquaintance that she is drawn to the hero by a force she cannot explain and the reader cannot believe (also, but less commonly, seen as **The Perfume Commercial**).

I'm a Pepper, Too!
This is a world in which all the characters share the same libertarian sentiments; everyone listens to awesome jam band Phish; everyone solves personal problems through crystal therapy . . .

Stag Night
The male author unthinkingly creates a world in which every single member of society is male except—hey presto!—when the protagonist feels like getting laid. Especially common in science fiction; apparently many writers assume that in the future women will die out.

The Country Club

Here every single character is white and middle to upper class. Unless your novel is taking place in rural Sweden, this will eventually give the reader an eerie feeling that some form of ethnic cleansing has taken place.

The Diane Arbus Retrospective

Here Earth is populated entirely by the grotesque and unhappy, the deformed and downtrodden. Every encounter is a chance to meet another mean-spirited bully or debased drug-fiend hooker. This world has a strict dress code: all clothing must be garish, ill-fitting, and/or stained. For reasons we cannot fathom, the natives of such worlds spend a lot of time on mass transportation.

14

RESEARCH AND HISTORICAL BACKGROUND

"Call my patent attorney!" cried Thomas Edison. "I have invented the telephone!"

As the unpublished writer sits down to begin his epic novel about the campaigns of Genghis Khan he realizes he can go one of two ways. The first is to put in hours of painstaking research, whose fruits he will deftly integrate into his story, making it vivid and uncannily real. Here is the other.

"Hello! I Am the Medieval Knight!"

In which characters supply their own context

The samurai sheathed his sword and reposed on the rice mat, crossing his legs in the accepted manner. The geisha smiled at him, strumming her ikebana gracefully.

"Ah, Tamiko," he said. "Tomorrow I make war, as is the way of the samurai. And if we do not prevail, ironic though it seems, I shall take my own life, as to do otherwise would be considered a shameful blot upon the entire Wagamama Clan."

"Yes," she said, smiling gracefully. "You will make the incision to the west, then the northwest, then to the east, as your forefathers also did in the case of defeat."

"But," he said with a roguish smile, "At least in our culture the pleasures of the flesh are not frowned upon, as I hear is customary among the barbarians of the mysterious West. Here if I wish to enjoy a woman, no shame is connected with that fact."

The geisha made a graceful grimace. "Alas!" she said. "I am, however, a victim of the double standard imposed by this paternalistic society. Due to the stigma placed on my traditional vocation, I can never expect to make a respectable marriage—even though the geisha are highly educated in the graceful arts, and are not mere prostitutes."

This version of "Hello! I Am the Mommy!" (page 145) presents characters obsessively discussing the values and norms of their own culture. The Vikings explain Viking customs to each other at every turn, despite never having met anyone who wasn't a Viking.

A variation on this is the rebellious protagonist who questions the never-before questioned values of a society, from the point of view of the author's never-questioned contemporary American values. While up to a certain point (the heroine who chafes at the restrictions of Victorian respectability, say) this device is accepted by readers, be sure the rebellious stance is one that *could* arise in the world of the novel.

One workable tactic is to introduce a foreigner into the

Vikings' midst and exploit the mutual misunderstandings to address the specifics of their respective cultures. The Vikings can then explain their culture without straining credulity.

Historical Fiction and the Challenge of the Strange

When writing any novel set in a world that the reader is not familiar with, whether it is the land of Faerie, an alien planet, or the Mongol empire, the writer must do more heavy lifting than he would if the novel were set last year in Anytown, USA.

You can say that a scene is set in Times Square on New Year's Eve, 1999, and there is already a picture in your reader's head. Tell the reader that the action is taking place on the planet Nebulon Prime, during the height of Xinth season, and he is still looking at a blank canvas. The further from the world that the reader knows, the more construction the writer must do. America in 1914 will require a fair amount of embroidery, but not as much as Italy in 1514. China in 914 will require thousands of extra words of explanation of local customs, costumes, buildings, etc.

Where specifics are lacking, the reader will unconsciously fill in any missing details with the minutiae of his own world. If you say that Galdor of Nebulon sat down to breakfast, and do not describe any of the elements of that breakfast, the reader who eats Froot Loops every morning will on some level understand Galdor to be doing the same.

While science fiction or fantasy requires that the writer create a world that is consistent and believable, historical fiction requires that it also be right. To this end, some authors manage to fit entire courses in medieval society or Chinese military history into their novels. Where this works, it is a bonus prized by readers; but in order to work, the historical writing needs to be executed at least as well as popular nonfiction, and in a similar manner.

A device frequently used to ground the reader in the historical period of the novel is the cameo, in which the everyman protagonist meets Charlemagne, Queen Victoria, or Benjamin Franklin, the one person from that time and place of whom the reader has heard. This can work when the bastard son's introduction at court, or the orphan's apprenticeship at Benjamin Franklin's print shop, is the subject of the novel. If they serve no greater function in your novel than a montage of the Eiffel Tower, the Arc de Triomphe, and a baguette serves at the beginning of a movie, chances are they should be replaced.

Above all, when the author herself finds history boring, her historical novel suffers. Since she skipped any and all passages of historical exposition in her favorite novels, she's decided she would be doing the reader a favor by omitting them in the book she is writing. Though her book is set in Tudor England, she does not mention, because she does not know, anything about what kind of government England had, what people did for a living, and whether they believed in Jesus Christ or Zoroaster. In some cases she deals with this by omitting any mention of the setting; in others she cobbles together a setting from vague memories of *Xena: Warrior Princess*.

Historical research has the same status as all background information. The author must know it, even if it does not appear directly in the novel. Otherwise, the characters won't seem like people, and the setting won't seem like a place.

Zeno's iPod:
Anachronism in Historical Fiction

Plato took out a pencil, opened his notebook, and started a new Dialogue.

Pocahontas unhooked her bra and winked mischievously at John Smith.

"Are you going to finish that sandwich?" the centurion asked.

Most beginning novelists start out with a setting that is reasonably close to home, and the mundane details—what people eat, what they wear, what they do with potatoes—are at their fingertips. Once the novelist starts to wander into periods long ago and far away, though, things often go very very wrong. Sure, everybody knows that knights don't carry guns, Julius Caesar did not drive to the Senate, and medieval doctors prescribed leeches, not Viagra. But sometimes a paper clip, a paperback, or a cherry lollipop will find its way into Charlemagne's court. And while the author has somehow managed to overlook this inconsistency, no reader, whatever his degree of historical ignorance, will.

Always check and recheck for anachronistic details. A single stray basketball can squash your whole carefully constructed Viking saga.

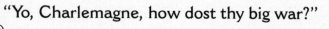

"Yo, Charlemagne, how dost thy big war?"

When the author does not control his idiom

"So, Signor Michelangelo, how does the ceiling prosper?" Pope Sixtus asked, strolling into the chapel.

Michelangelo didn't answer at first. His back was aching fearfully, after his many hours painting in the awkward position the work required. He didn't trust himself to be polite. But at last he rolled onto his side and regarded the aging pope with an attempt at a polite smile. "Good morrow, Your Holiness. It's going."

The pope smiled as he prepared to broach the difficult subject. Though he personally felt this artist had pretensions beyond his station, he had a loathing for unseemly confrontations. "And have we anything like a completion date?"

Michelangelo snorted ironically, immediately losing his composure. "You people! Whine, whine, whine! Can't you see I'm breaking my ass up here?"

All fans of *Bill and Ted's Excellent Adventure* are familiar with the fun that can result when a Greek philosopher employs the language of contemporary New Jersey. Where the anachronism is unintentional, however, the only result is embarrassment. And that anachronism can result not just from things that *are* modern but from anything with a modern taste. It's certainly reasonable to think that King John might have suffered from depression, but just once say "King John felt depressed" and the entire structure of modern psychology is dragged into the thirteenth century.

The problem of anachronism in language is far more difficult to solve than the problem of anachronistic physical objects. You can easily remove an object, but all too often, in trying to keep language true to period, authors end up with something unnatural and stilted. "Forsooth, how does my lady in these recent turbulations of the realm?" is no more convincing than "How are you doing with everything that's going on, Lady Macbeth?"

The only solution to this problem is to study both literature written *during* the period you're addressing, and fiction written about the period by contemporary authors whom you trust. Then, revise and revise until you strike a happy medium.

The Whatchamacallit

In which gaps in the author's research make themselves known

The architect admired the way the building was crafted; it was all stone with curvy arches like an old church.

The physicist squinted into the microscope. This kind of atom was a tricky customer.

But I have an Army at my disposal! the president suddenly remembered. He got Congress on the phone and told him to declare war.

If you are going to write a character with specialized knowledge you yourself do not possess, particularly a character whose chief characteristic is possession of that specialized knowledge, you must take steps to avoid getting that knowledge wrong. Every profession has its own jargon, and names for the things commonly encountered; when your character encounters one of those things, it should be expressed in his terms, not yours.

Your landscape architect would cite the exact thing she is planting, rather than "lots of pretty flowers." Your coroner character observes "a slightly enlarged liver, showing some necrotic tissue" when she opens a body, not "sick organs."

This does not mean that you must qualify as a research biologist in order to write about one. But do not have your research biologist refer to the "nasty germs" she is studying. As always, it is a good idea for the author to know more than he shows, so while reading popular material on your subject is a good start, it won't hurt to dip into more specialized materials so you have more of a feel for the subject.

Maybe you won't understand *exactly* how a polymerase chain reaction works, but you'll know enough not to have a character drink a pint of polymerase chain reaction to cure his rabies.

Then Mel Gibson Raised His Mighty Broadsword!

In which the author unconsciously appropriates

And so I watched the unsinkable ocean liner surrender itself to the icy deep. It was a clear night, the stars all atwinkle, as if tiny shards of the fearsome Berg had flown upwards and lodged in the heavens as it scraped and tore at the side of the mighty ship. It was the unsheathed arrogance of this, the Gilded Age, that made us think we could build a craft that was unsinkable, even while we were blind to the teeming masses crammed into steerage. Many of them would drown soon because cowardly uncaring crew members would not stop to unlock the many gates that kept them below.

I could picture, for example, a mother lying down in her berth with her two little children, calming them as the chill of the encroaching seawater crept ever higher. Others ran and stampeded like the animals the rich thought them to be, but later, on the upper decks, the wellborn showed themselves a mixed lot as well, some fearless and noble, sacrificing themselves to helping others while wearing elegant evening clothes, while one in particular schemed to get aboard a lifeboat. He even went so far as to drape himself with a shawl and try to pass for a woman. It was a lesson, I suppose, as to the weakness of the rich, who thought they knew the price of everything but truly knew the value of nothing, including paintings by visionary painters that would someday be valuable.

While all of us, save academic historians (and perhaps even they) unconsciously put together our picture of the past out of bits and pieces floating around in the cultural stew, you should not limit your research to Blockbuster. Though some readers will have missed that movie about King George, others will instantly recognize the scenes and details you have purloined from it. Sometimes such thefts are unconscious, so it's worth pausing to consider whether those velvet curtains that get turned into a dress by the desperate Southern belle—the turning point of your book!—might ring bells of another kind in the reader's mind.

Class Struggle

*Wherein the author struggles to
imagine an unfamiliar class*

"How do you do, sir?" said the dowager imperiously, allowing her hand to be kissed by Sebastian Skeaping, insurance salesman to the rich. Butlers clustered by the door, looking immaculate in their white gloves and top hats. Just then, a delivery boy pushed his way through the crowd, presenting the dowager's daughter, the heiress, with a diamond tiara.

"Ooh! C'est from the Marquis de London!" the girl squealed in excitement, and then slapped the delivery boy for daring to look at her. Then she thought better of it and made plans to run off with him because she was of an age to want adventures among the rabble. Her daydream was interrupted by Skeaping, who insinuated himself to her side. "Mademoiselle," he said smoothly. "Shouldn't you have that covered against theft? The Cat Burglar has been spotted recently prowling the Penthouses of Manhattan Island."

*   *   *

Meanwhile, on the other side of the tracks, Flip and Slappy lit their pot cigarettes. They were sitting in their crack house, where roaches and termites crawled among piles of dirty needles. "Hot damn!" said Slappy. "That horse is kicking my butt!"

Flip laughed and picked up the bag of white powders from the floor. "You got that right, soul brother!" he exclaimed. "This is the hardest drug I ever toked!"

In the century since writers like Scott Fitzgerald and Edith Wharton wrote their novels of class observation, Americans have embraced the idea of social mobility and a classless society. While we won't debate the truth or politics of these ideas, experience suggests that class differences persist and, in fact, are among the hardest to see past.

Research can tell us the physical details that make up the lives of people we haven't encountered, but the feelings and attitudes that guide them through their worlds are not so easily discerned. We will either assume that other people think as we do, or apply ideas we have unconsciously cobbled together from television shows and old movies. The way people in a particular subculture interact, their unspoken assumptions and etiquette, are also difficult to glean from books, and readers will immediately spot a sham in this respect.

If you have only ever seen a duke on television, everything your fictional duke does, says, wears, or thinks becomes an opportunity to demonstrate that you have never met a duke. If you have never served time in prison, chances are that your prison will feel more like your workplace with a greater emphasis on group showers than it will an actual prison.

The most effective kinds of research into social settings are either time spent *in* those settings or immersion in what historians call primary sources—books, accounts, and documents generated by members of that group.

The Research Paper

In which the author overdoes it

The research biologist sat on the park bench and tried to collect her thoughts. She gazed at the grass that shone in the sun. Though to the eye of the average person, it would seem as if nothing was going on, she knew that 10^{24}

molecules of CO_2 were being converted to glucose and oxygen every second in the humble-appearing organisms. But the glories of the Calvin cycle, and the further intricacies of the Krebs cycle, essential to cellular respiration, were little comfort now that her husband, Hugh, had bonked that secretary, in an act of sexual congress whose origins lay in a reproductive innovation evolved in algae 2.7 million years ago!

Thank you for doing that research we asked you to do. We know it was hard, and probably parts of it were boring. Other parts were absolutely fascinating—and naturally you want to share that experience of doors being opened, of knowledge flooding into your mind, with your reader. But beware.

Conceivably your coroner character, by virtue of being a coroner, would look at a barista and see a stack of organs waiting to be unzipped. And perhaps she would describe this experience to herself with a long concatenation of Latin terms. But more likely she would only see a source of frappuccino and would describe this to herself in terms of "Can I afford the calories?" like anyone else.

Confine the fruits of your research to passages in which specialized knowledge is necessary and appropriate. While we do not want your astronomer to look at the night sky and see "pretty lights," we also do not want him to be reminded of the mathematics governing the formation of galaxies every time he stirs his coffee.

15

THEME

*Gregor Samsa awoke one morning to find himself
turned into an enormous symbol.*

Ah, theme! How it inspires! It is the ghost in the machine, the
chewy nougat at the center of the pecan log, the cart before the
horse. What unpublished author can resist the siren call of the
soapbox? Below we show you how to pack your novel with such a
high density of meaning that it will form a black hole from which
no story can ever escape.

The Overture

*Wherein the prologue is a brief guide
—————————to the meaning of life*

Prologue

Life is fate. The world is one—and many. No one can tell
when our world will end or even if it has an end, a begin-

ning, or a middle. We can only go with the flow and hope
for the children.

A man is born. He creeps through life on his metaphorical hands and knees, seeking—ever seeking. Seeking. Only to die with that question still on his lips: what
is it that I seek?

In the ages since Earth was formed from the sweepings
from the Big Firework that made our so-called universe,
generations have risen and been consigned to the scrap
heap, all straining to become themselves without ever
truly knowing if those selves were selves or simply the
clowns or dreams of space and time. Will the mishmash
of eternity ever be unknotted by the laser of conscious-
ness? Only we hold the answer—if we do.

But as Niestchze said, "For every thing there is a
season." Thus begins the season of Harry Carruthers:
insurance salesman, father, lover, and seeker, ever
seeking.

You're writing a story about a man who cheats on his wife with
the babysitter and ends up losing his marriage, children, home,
and babysitter. But it's not just about him—it's about all of us.
In fact, it's about the human condition, and perhaps—though it
may be immodest to say so—the meaning of the universe. So
what better way to set the stage than to write a profound prologue to your story about the link between Harry, the universe,
and everything?

The problem here is that as far as the reader is concerned, you're
just some guy with an opinion. At this point, you're the drunk on
the next barstool, asking nobody in particular "You wanna know
wha' my philosophy is? Well, I'll tell ya . . ." You have not yet
bought the reader's respect and interest in what you think; you

have not yet drawn your reader into a world in which that philosophy has a crucial impact on what happens next in the plot.

We paid our money to be entertained, not lectured to. Your beliefs might be intriguing and enlightening, but if that was what we wanted to read, we'd have been shopping in nonfiction.

The Timely Epiphany

In which symbols conveniently make themselves known

Vivian's thoughts were a lumpy stew as she inched the car along the Long Island Expressway. She'd worked late, and a pang of guilt shot through her. Could she be a good mother and still have a career as a media buyer? At the sharp honk from the car to her right she looked over and saw the balding, overweight, middle-aged man behind the wheel. His face was red and sweaty, and he looked like a candidate for the same heart attack that had taken her Mort, leaving her with the weight of the world on her shapely and well-exercised shoulders.

She would resist becoming like that. She refused to give up her nurturing qualities as a woman, despite the crude and vulgar men she competed with. Just then she passed the billboard for Roger's Dairy, and she glowed with pride—there were smiling children with milk moustaches holding out their glasses for more. She had placed that ad there, over the objection of the men in her office.

Maybe it was no coincidence that she had won the milk account. Maybe it was no coincidence that her name was Vivian, which meant life. She suddenly realized that Mort, the name of her dead husband, meant death. Yes, the old way of doing business, men's way, it was death.

The world of media buying was opening up to women now. With their new, more nurturing way of doing things, media buying would change, and she, Vivian, was a part of it, and it was a part of her, a part of what she had to give her children as a mother. Yes, she thought, and I can be both a mother and a media buyer. If only her kids would understand.

Just then, her cell phone rang, and she turned on the speakerphone. It was her kids.

"We love you, mom!"

It is satisfying when plot and theme work together to provide an epiphany; when the struggles of the hero lead to a change in perspective that makes it all worth while for both us and the character. However, when the symbols that trigger that epiphany are too baldly placed in the character's path for her to trip over, we are not so much satisfied as annoyed.

Symbols and action should not be one-to-one, and they should not be standing right next to each other, a neat double line in which each character or action holds hands with his symbol-buddy, marching through your novel in lockstep. Above all, symbols should not be obvious. While a novel cannot do without plot or characters, your novel should work perfectly well for someone who doesn't notice the symbols at all.

The Fig Leaf

When the author has his cake and eats it

"And then this chick, the redhead with the amazing rack, like size XL breasts on this itty bitty chick, so you know she's gonna be that tight, dude, right?" Bob leered suggestively.

"Hm," I said, trying to appear interested. Little did he realize that his offensively chauvinist talk now disgusted me.

"And yeah, so I get her home and I tear her blouse right in half, but she's totally into it, she doesn't even care. And I'm chowing down on her tits, which are 100% bona fide flesh, no plastic paps, you get me? God, my dick's as hard as Chinese arithmetic."

I sighed and reluctantly sipped my beer. All around us in the tasteless club, girls strutted around with their large and lively boobs bobbing, barely concealed in filmy tank tops. Their miniskirts barely covered their voluptuous asses as they sashayed provocatively. Like Bob, they still lived in a world where all a woman had to offer was her body, where she couldn't be appreciated for her mind and capacities. I sighed as a girl smiled drunkenly at me, leaning forward to display her lush cleavage, a banquet of willing flesh for the taking—little did she know it was her mind that would have interested me!

Sometimes an author is torn between the desire to present certain material and a guilty awareness that others will not approve. In an attempt to deflect criticism, he apologizes as he goes, pointing out that the minstrel show, strip club visit, or cheap, all-purpose servants in a Third World setting are terribly, terribly distasteful to him, and he disapproves as much as anyone—more! Meanwhile, he continues to wallow in these scenes, exposing what everyone instantly recognizes as the world of his fantasies. The result is often reminiscent of a sixties sexploitation movie on the dangers of promiscuity.

It is best to assume that you are fooling nobody, because you are fooling nobody. If you are irresistibly drawn to exploitative material, you are far better off openly celebrating your sleaziness than using your fiction to stage a war between your id and your superego.

The Commercial Break

In which the author borrows

Jared walked away from his parents' house and got into the car with Shannon.

"What's wrong, dude?" she asked.

He shook his dreads in frustration. "It's just, you know, my parents. They're so, I don't know, just so—"

Just then he heard the perfect song come on the radio, the song that expressed it all.

"Hey! Crank that, okay?"

The two nodded in time to the music as they listened.

Dressed in your hypocrisy
The face you show
Doesn't know
We can see your eyes wide shut
You cannot see the lies we see
That rip our souls
Our childhood sold
For thirty coins of fool's gold

As the song wound down to its final chords, Shannon sighed and said, "It's so right for us, for now. It's like they know."

"That's it," Jared said. "They're expressing everything

about our parents, our dead society, and all that stuff. It's like it's about what we've been going through with that guidance counselor, totally."

"Yeah . . . Rage Against the Pumpkin rocks."

Sometimes, feeling that his own eloquence is inadequate to the task at hand, the author bows out gracefully and lets his character come across a poem, an Ayn Rand novel, or a quote from Martin Luther King's "I Have a Dream" speech to spell out the message for him. But the reader is not buying your book to find out what Ani DiFranco has to say about life. She expects *you* to have something to say about life, and to say it, because that is what we pay writers to do.

There are instances when quotes can work very well. These include plots that are in some way *about* music, poetry, etc., and where there is an interweaving between these and the characters' lives. Quotes can also work where the quoted material isn't stating the message but expanding or commenting on it obliquely, so the reader doesn't feel as if she's hearing a public service announcement for the book's theme. But when the quote is an on-the-nose statement of the message, it seems as if the writer wanted to take a day off and found a guest author to cover his shift.

The After-Dinner Sermon

In which the author wields a mallet

"No, you don't understand, Pueblo," Gruff said, keeping the gun trained on the shivering drug kingpin's forehead. "It's not just about what drugs do to people. It's about what money does to people. Money can be just like a drug. You would do anything for money, just as an addict would do anything for your cocaine. When money becomes more important than family, useful work, and community commitments, we've lost our bearings. That's why your relationships with women—however beautiful they are!—are finally shallow and unsatisfying."

"I theenk I hear envy in your voice, pendejo," said Pueblo Espadrille, sneering ironically.

"Ha!" laughed Gruff. "When you have sacrificed everything to money, you lose your ability to value those things. You think I envy your money, but in fact the only person I envy is the humble señorita you despise and maltreat. Though life has dealt her a cruel hand, she has maintained her dignity and her ability to love. She is the rich one, not you. It is the ability to love that makes us true kingpins of the cartel of humanity."

Like everyone else, characters have their philosophies of life. Sometimes the protagonist and the author share the same philosophy of life, and the protagonist expresses that philosophy for both of them. In moderation, this is a good thing. It can make the reader feel that it is not only the happiness of the characters that is at stake, but eternal values. It can also make the reader feel that the character is like a real companion, who shares her ideas about life as they while away the hours together. Alternatively, it can make the reader feel like someone is beating him over the head with a self-help manual.

Another point to keep in mind is that there is a higher standard for such pronouncements than for themes expressed by the actions of the characters. Ideas expressed directly should be original, witty, or genuinely insightful. While it's fine for the plot to exemplify the idea that "love conquers all," and readers will happily read book after book expressing no other theme than that, they are in it for the story. Have a character deliver a speech explaining that love conquers all, and our eyes glaze over. We all want to *see* love triumph, but not even the simplest among us wants a long explication of the idea that love is pretty darn potent.

The Educational Film

In which the deck is stacked

Rainflower entered the Starbucks reluctantly. She had been down by the river cleaning squirrels, victims of the latest Exxon oil spill, and, due to corporate decimation of the small local businesses, there was nowhere else to wash her hands. The bathroom door was locked, and she went to the counter for the key. The three baristas were gathered together, looking at her and sniggering.

"May I have the key to the bathroom?" she asked, in her sweetest voice. "I need to wash my hands."

"Oh, really?" said one girl, her nicotine breath wafting poisonously over Rainflower. "I didn't know hippies washed." The others cackled and high-fived. One kicked the key underneath the gigantic refrigerator, which seemed to leer malevolently with its freight of refined sugar and dairy, threatening millions of children with obesity.

Staggering back out, her hands burning with the military-industrial complex's oily toxins, Rainflower got back on her bicycle, the frame of which she had woven herself out of wicker, and started the long ride home. All the way, hostile car drivers cursed at her from their windows or even attempted to sideswipe her.

"You there! Stop!"

Rainflower saw the grossly fat, huffing cop waving at her and stopped her bicycle.

"Don't you know it's illegal to ride like that, slut?" he asked, and spat at her tire.

"Like what, officer?" she asked.

"Yeah, play dumb," he said and wrote her a bunch of tickets. As she stood, nearly crying with the pain of her poisoned hands, dead-eyed men in suits walked past, ogling her and nodding approvingly at the fascist cop.

This is a more comprehensive version of "The Fearless Exposé," (page 92) in which every character, situation, and setting is calculated to express a single political injustice. Books like these are sometimes published by special-interest presses, where everyone involved is devoted to expressing the viewpoint concerned. This is not to say that they are read.

If you want to reach a wide audience, start by openly acknowledging that the novel is designed mainly to illustrate the wrong in question. Then choose vignettes over the course of months or years, so that the long series of injustices remains plausible.

To take a common example, here we are in the days of Hitler's regime, monitoring the growing persecution of the Jews. But we do not simply follow Tevye on his way to work and have him persecuted in eighteen different ways by every German he passes. We follow him through several months, seeing the changing situation illustrated through the experience of various characters. Sometimes Tevye is one of them, and sometimes he learns about it secondhand. And just occasionally, Tevye is forgetting his troubles in Fievel's arms.

Sometimes an unpublished author will stake out a position that is shared by everybody else in the world and defend it as if he stood embattled and alone. As he stridently argues with what he seems to think of as a recalcitrant audience that it is bad to be unkind to animals, the reader balks and eventually rebels. Yes, you have a point—but why are you shouting at *us?*

Another possibility is a novel that expresses a belief with which *no one* agrees. These can be broken down into three broad categories:

The High Colonic by Mail

In which the author's worldview
does not intersect with the reader's

Before I left the house, I did my usual exercises, adding a few repetitions of "Calling Up Anus Energy" and "Forklift." After washing the instruments, I headed out to the precinct, confidently awash in the vax energy the exercises had released from the structure of my house, which I had chosen for its geomantic properties.

At the corner of 88th and Broadway, a woman stopped dead as I was walking by, stunned by the power of my presence. To my surprise, she turned out to be one of the Elected. Fixing me with her hazel and violet eyes, she commanded, "Lord of the Upper Eighties, yield!" Then I knew I would spend the next hour not, as I had planned, solving the Kapolski murder, but delivering my vax to this vixenish Electedess by means of the Heinlein Interpenetration.

There are many different paths in life. Sometimes the path we choose takes us far, far from the main road. And a good thing, too: where would we be if we all agreed? However, in a commercial novel for the general public, it is advisable to stop and consider whether most readers will share our beliefs about the world.

Yes, surely someday "vax" will be a household word. But the way to hasten that day is not to write as if it has already arrived. If you are far from the mainstream, a more gently persuasive approach is called for.

Sometimes, it is just a single idea that is jarringly out of place:

Obsession, by Calvin Klein (you know he's Jewish, right?)

When the author is unaware that his idée fixe is showing

"Why don't you give me a call sometime? We could get dinner," the girl said, smiling coyly. She began to jot down her phone number on a cocktail napkin.

As she frowned in concentration, my heart sank. She was just another one of these slutty girls who would sleep with anyone—they couldn't help themselves. It wasn't that they enjoyed sex, either; women got no more pleasure from the sex act than I would from scratching a mosquito bite. It was sheer egotism, an endless craving to be seen as "attractive." In fact, these sluts were usually secret lesbians.

Maybe you've never threaded a ribbon of cotton muslin through your alimentary canal while chanting "Vax! Vax!" but you do have one fiercely held belief that creeps into everything you write.

It may even be that the opinion you hold is not uncommon,

but the ferocity with which you hold it is. Many novels allude to the duplicity of women, but few mention it on every page. When it becomes a recurring motif, it can be disconcerting enough to alienate the reader and inspire his mistrust. It can seem as if the writer is constructing his entire fictional universe in order to sneak in a propaganda pitch.

Uncommon opinions should be presented sparingly, and cut altogether if the reader will be able to think of nothing else. They are also best presented as opinions, not inarguable truths. Remember that if you set out to tell a story, your real aim is to tell a story, not to expose the hypocrisy of the tenure system, the grave dangers of the unnecessary root canal, the merits of universal daylight savings time . . .

The Voice in the Wilderness

Wherein the view expressed is universally detested

The Commandant wept as he let go the dying Jewess's hand. Despite the best efforts of the SS doctors, and the guards who had volunteered to work overtime tending the ill, so many of the poor inmates at Auschwitz were succumbing to the typhus from which their caregivers had tried to protect them. The guards were even being forced to burn the bodies rather than giving them a proper burial. Of course, the predictable reports in the Allied papers of "death camps" continued.

He trembled with rage as he thought of how he and his men had gone without food so that the ailing prisoners could eat, and how they had been demonized for it.

Someday, he thought, someday their sacrifices would be known!

Perhaps you believe it with all your heart. Perhaps you feel the facts have been systematically suppressed by special interest groups or the CIA. Perhaps you feel your novel will be the one that blows the lid off that conspiracy and lets readers finally know the *truth*.

Or maybe you think a crazy, iconoclastic view will help to sell your book. How about a world where children *love* pedophiles? You can't buy publicity like that. Copies will fly off the shelves.

No. Whether you are expressing a private conviction or just being shocking, you will never make it to the shelves. An editor might sit up and take notice, but only because he knows that while it only takes a minute to reject your novel, he will be dining out on the story of how repellent you are for years to come.

PART VI

—

SPECIAL EFFECTS AND NOVELTY ACTS— DO NOT TRY THIS AT HOME

"How did I get to be the protagonist? Easy! I fucked the author!"

Some might feel we have been unnecessarily discouraging to this point. We hope you will understand that this has been nothing more than tough love. If we have been harsh, it is our way of encouraging you to do your very best as you go about the difficult task of writing your novel.

We come now, however, to material where "doing your best" is just not good enough. We come to an area so rife with peril that it would be irresponsible of us to do anything but baldly plead with you to turn back now.

When it comes to sex, jokes, and postmodernism, the subjects we are now about to discuss, we must insist that if you can't do something right, give up. Give up and do something else, because, frankly, a poorly executed sex scene or an unfunny joke is of less value than no sex scene or no joke, and the conventions of postmodernism poorly handled are the quickest route up one's own ass.

Giving a reader a sex scene that is only half right is like giving her half of a kitten. It is not half as cute as a whole kitten; it is a bloody, godawful mess. A half-right sex scene is not half as hot; it actually moves into the negative numbers, draining any heat from the surrounding material.

A joke that falls flat is not just a joke that the reader does not laugh at; it is a drain on your supply of goodwill. It will disincline your reader to laugh at your next joke, and with each failed joke, it is less likely that the reader will make it to the one in Chapter Eleven that works.

Failed postmodernism is not a half-brilliant, half-hilarious, tour de half-force; it looks as if the author's hard drive had been turned upside down and shaken like an Etch A Sketch, randomly mixing together bits and pieces of fiction, correspondence, and workout diaries.

Any of the following crimes against fiction can prevent the publication of your novel. Committing several will prevent the publication of novels by anyone whose name is similar to yours, just in case.

SEX SCENES

The Hays Code

Where the author looks away

The fierce pirate pressed her to the deck and laughed as he tore away her clothes. "Struggle all you like, my pretty!" he cried. "Thou'll not escape my clutches now!"

Some time later, she felt herself released from his iron grip. She was alive and safe, but—oh, mother!—no longer a virgin. And what was worse, she was in love!

Sometimes the reader is really in it for the cheap thrills. There is no point writing a steamy sexploitation novel if you cannot bring yourself to peek at the dirty bits. The days when Rhett Butler carried Scarlett up the stairs (fade to black) and then the sun rose the next day are gone with the wind.

When to Kiss and Tell

Unless your genre is porn, any sex act that has no plot significance attached to it should be examined carefully. Sometimes it's exactly what's needed to give richness to the relationships, make the pacing a little more leisurely, or just add sauce. And sometimes it's like getting embarrassing spam. Making that judgment call is so complicated that we cannot offer guidelines that will serve in every situation. But here are some of the issues to consider.

• Does the sex scene advance the plot or backstory in any way? This doesn't have to mean that sleeping with her karate coach will change the heroine's life forever. It could be something much more minimal—perhaps the karate coach is the one who gives her the confidence to go back and confront Pollutio Manufacturing Inc. about that suspicious coelacanth bloom in Fetid Creek. Or perhaps something he tells her about life in Japan gives her the clue she needs to solve the Kapolski murder. If you can work any of these things in, it may make your sex scene less gratuitous. However, an utter, complete, shameless, gratuitous scene can also work . . . except where it doesn't. Your conscience (or your bluntest friend) must be the judge.

• Has a sex scene that is almost identical happened before? By "almost identical" we chiefly mean the same characters having sex in the same circumstances. While newlyweds having sex is a great scene, with repetition it becomes **The Second Fellatio in the Laundromat,** and boring. It does not help if they try a daring new position. But it may if they are doing it in steerage on the Titanic while the boat sinks.

• A good time *not* to write a sex scene is when you don't really want to. Most genres can thrive without any explicit sex at all, and if you are uncomfortable writing it, we are liable to be uncomfortable reading it (see "Assembly Instructions," page 230, for the likely outcome).

• Scenes where a bad guy is given a creepy fetish in order to establish his depravity are less and less of a good idea. In a time when fetishes are becoming a must-have for the really hip urban professional, you are likely to be stepping on the toes of many readers by using Nefaro's bondage thing as short-hand for Evil. The key is that Nefaro should be a rotten, inconsiderate boor to his girlfriend, not that he is a rotten, inconsiderate boor to his girlfriend who sometimes ties her up.

Dear Penthouse Letters

Wherein the reader is offered no foreplay

Cinderella's breath came more quickly as her Prince pulled aside the gossamer curtains that curtained the bed diaphanously. She could hear the twitter of the blue-birds just outside the window, which looked out on a soft green landscape bathed in the warming light of the setting sun.

She smiled at him as he lay beside her, and she could see all their many tomorrows bringing her happiness such as she felt right now. His hand on her shoulder pushed aside her dressing gown to reveal her pendulous breasts, and then he guided her hand to his angry throbbing dick.

"Suck me," he demanded and her head bobbed juicily, eager to please.

Desire is a funny thing. It can take on many wondrous forms. The porn form, complete with standard epithets and obligatory adjectives, has its uses.

But it has a distinctive tone, which does not mesh well with most love scenes. If the main point of the scene is consummated *love,* not *lust,* the author should focus on feelings and touches, not on boob shape and penis rigidity. In fact, too much emphasis on these things may give the sense that the author is a third person in the room, a voyeur leering at the lovers' tender love-making.

And even when the scene is not tender and dreamy but downright filthy, there should be a transition from the language of everyday life to the language of rock-hard, cum-splattered filth. While sex and humor are both very difficult to realize on the page, it is all too easy to realize humor while trying to realize sex. Letting your lovers engage in a certain amount of foreplay will help to ensure that when you get to the act itself, the reader is ready to take the word "throbbing" in the spirit in which it is meant.

The Superhuman Feat

Wherein a man performs

> He lifted the naked chorus girl into the air and plunged her
> down, impaling her on his rock-hard dick. She squealed
> as she immediately came one—two—three—four—five
> times! He continued lifting her and lowering her with
> his strong arms, fucking her long after she had lost con-
> sciousness from sheer pleasure. As he approached an
> earth-shattering orgasm, he couldn't help congratulating
> himself: not bad for a fifty-year-old who was having his
> tenth screw of the night!

People certainly vary in their native capacities. Some people can
carry a heavy suitcase upstairs without breaking a sweat. Some
can do backflips, walk on their hands, or juggle flaming swords.
Some people can even recite poetry in public without losing their
dignity. But there are some things *no one alive* can do.

In the past, this kind of hyperbole was accepted—in the
novels, for instance, of Harold Robbins—written in an age
before people discussed sex, and everybody assumed that this
must be what everybody else was doing.

Assembly Instructions

In which the sex is drained of sex

> He handled first her left, then her right, breast. Then she
> stroked his back and he stroked hers. Then they did that
> again. They took off their clothes, and she hung hers up,

while he folded his carefully and put them on the chair by the closet. He said "Excuse me" and used the bathroom, and remembered to spray room freshener before he left. When he was done he went back into the bedroom, where she lay naked on the bed. He walked to the bed and looked at the different parts of her body, starting from the bottom: feet, ankles, knees, crotch, midriff, bosom. She put her legs further apart to allow penetration, so he penetrated her.

Sometimes it's just too hard to make yourself type those dirty words. Pondering what will happen when your grandmother reads your book, you decide that "penis" is the standard term. But what is the hero doing with it? Well, not fucking—that's kind of . . . vulgar, isn't it? What would a doctor say? He'd use Latin words, like "copulate."

That's it! Now you can unflinchingly describe what your characters are doing, but without being unseemly.

The result will be something that sounds like a medical brochure about erectile dysfunction. What's more, it will read as more perverse than a straightforward "They fucked all night," and in a disturbing, Norman Bates-y way.

You are better off cutting out the sex altogether if you're going to turn the lovers' tryst into an "act of intercourse."

The Purple Blue Prose

In which the sex is cloaked in lyricism

As he unzipped, Hugh's tumid penis sprang to freedom like a Jack-in-the-Box. At first it seemed to approve its liberty, nodding affirmatively like a gamesome horse. But almost immediately it wanted to run to ground again. Like a vampire who feared the touch of sunlight, it dove for the nearest dark corner, dragging Hugh behind it. Hugh had become a mere appendage to a runaway sex organ, which dove into Virginia's lightless cranny with no fear of what beasts might lurk there. And beasts, Hugh was certain, there would be. How many tight corners Hugh had found himself in as a result of his unruly member's enthusiasm for spelunking!

Most descriptions of sex are so unimaginative, aren't they? The same stale four-letter words, the same predictable acts. Well, you're not going to be some boring old hack! You're going to dress it up with a metaphorical structure that will be witty, insightful, and poetic all at once. Maybe it will even include a few crafty puns.

Unfortunately, flowery, metaphorical treatments of sex almost always go wrong. In fact, just about the only case where they won't go wrong is where the author is intentionally making fun of a character for his pretentious attitude during the act in question.

JOKES

The Newborn Dinosaur

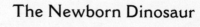
Where the reader, and everyone else, has heard that one before

"Well, she's a nice girl, and I like her a lot," Joe said. Then he made a face. "But she's kind of what I call a JAP."

"A Jap? She's not Japanese. She's Jewish, right?" Anna squinted in puzzlement.

"No, J—A—P. It stands for Jewish American Princess."

Anna burst out laughing. "Jewish American Princess! That's so perfect!"

Sometimes the author represents his characters in the act of inventing a joke that was old before Simon met Schuster. When a character uses comic material or witty idioms that almost everyone knows, the other characters should not be surprised and delighted; they will have heard it, too.

A Confederacy of Shills

Wherein characters laugh disproportionately

Joe concluded, "So that's how I earned my first million. If only I had known where it would lead!"

"Yeah, I guess it's a case of—mo' money, mo' troubles," said Elaine.

They both burst into unrestrained laughter. When Joe had gotten control of himself, he quipped, "Maybe I was better off as a po' boy!"

That set them off again. Elaine wiped tears of mirth from her eyes and managed, through gales of laughter, "Better off being an ordinary working stiff!"

"Stiff is right!" Joe said, making Elaine completely lose control. She yelped, "Stiff as a stiff!" getting her revenge by making Joe lose control, too. The laughter ricocheted and rebounded around the room for long hilarious minutes.

Even when the jokes are in fact funny, having your characters burst into gales of laughter at them tends to destroy the witty effect. It amounts to the author yukking it up over his own jokes, and has precisely the opposite effect that a laugh track does on a sitcom.

When the jokes are *not* funny, the reader is left with a bizarre dislocated feeling—just as if the characters were to weep for no reason, or run amok breaking the furniture for no reason.

It's usually best to err on the side of caution and have your characters laugh only occasionally and modestly. The laughter, most importantly, should not be there to show that the joke was funny (we'll make up our own minds about that) but to show some kind of bonding between the characters, or that they're having a good time, etc.

The Sight Gag

In which there is a sight gag

Jimmy came into the office wearing a baseball cap and a checked shirt with ill-fitting pants that were in a different check altogether. Adding to the comical effect, he walked with his heels turned out, pigeon-toed. All the while, his face had a goofy, hopeful expression.

"Hey, Mimi. Can I see the boss?" Jimmy asked. But before the receptionist could answer, he'd stepped on the end of his untied shoelace, and tripped with a wild flailing of his arms. First he kicked over an umbrella stand, causing the umbrellas to fly out. A few opened in midair. Batting the umbrellas away from his face, he fell on his butt and also knocked a heavy paperweight off the desk, which landed painfully on his testicles. Finally he scrambled back up to his feet, only to slip on an umbrella and land smack in the receptionist's lap.

Sight gags do not work in fiction, for the very good reason that you can't see them. Physical humor can still occasionally work, but the emphasis then is generally on the witty treatment of the fictional voice. If you don't think you can make a witty voice work, do not try to replace it with whoopie-cushion scenes.

You Should Also Avoid

The Fart Joke
Or the overflowing toilet joke, the nose-blowing joke, or any of their relations (see "The Unruly Zit," page 127).

The Size Joke
Wherein a woman has more than medium-sized breasts, or a man has a very large (or small) body part. While a good joke can be built around these things—or anything else—their presence does not make any joke automatically funny. Nor does

The Fat Lady
In fact, we strongly recommend that you avoid jokes whose main point is to ridicule a person whose weight, attractiveness, or other physical quality varies comically from the norm. It is ungenerous and ignoble, which should be enough to dissuade you, but if you are not looking to us for lessons in graciousness, we will point out that you will alienate any overweight, unattractive, etc., readers. And remember that unlike writers, editors are not always slim and fetching.

Finally, make sure you're not channeling

The *Seinfeld* Episode

All too many comic scenes in novels are disturbingly familiar. This is because they have been lifted from the author's lifetime of sitcom and movie watching. Since there will be some people reading your work who never saw that episode where Elaine dates the wrestling coach, there will always be people who think the stolen scene is brilliant. And it was, when Jerry Seinfeld and Larry David wrote it. The reproduction, whether conscious or unconscious, will seem markedly less brilliant when read by somebody who also saw that episode.

POSTMODERNISM

"Hello! I Am the Author!"

Where the novel is self-referential

The Blank Page
by Newton Showalter

Newton Showalter sat at his desk facing a blank page.[1]
What has brought me, Newton thought, to spend all

---

1 While the name of the author of this novel and the character he writes about would appear to be the same, they are pronounced differently, and they did not even get along the one time they met.[2]

2 Gainsville, Florida, March 18, 1984.

my time creating fictional worlds that only I will ever enter, having the habit, as I do, of deleting anything I might have written at the end of every day?[3]

I shall make a list, Newton Showalter quickly determined, to define the barriers to speaking. Here then, the list Newton Showalter made, which I can assure you is reproduced accurately.[4]

- As a postcolonial white male, I assume the creative impulse is something to be waved about, like a penis.
- Late capitalism is .mhy76bgtvfs—hold on, my pesky cat, Bartok Showalter, just walked across the keyboard, ironically disrupting yet again the suspension of disbe . . .

---

3   How then could you be reading this, reader? Could it be that the narrator of this tale is not accurately reporting the thoughts of Newton Showalter? Or could it be that you yourself are Newton Showalter?

4   While fiction is traditionally an exalted type of lying, and reading is therefore a prolonged disbelief, here you can put aside any such misgivings for a number of reasons, which I will list as soon as I'm done with the list coming up . . . right . . . *now!*

For the purposes of this discussion, postmodernism will be defined as any conscious reference to the author as the author, the novel as a novel, writing as little ink shapes on paper, or anything else that underlines the artificial nature of fiction.

It should be immediately obvious that all these things are baldly inimical to the novelist's goal of writing a story that the reader can believe in.

Why then do people keep writing novels in which the author is a character, bizarre footnotes intrude, and typographic tricks remind us of the book as a physical object, which might easily be shied at the head of a smarty-pants writer?

Because, every year, someone gets away with it. That person gets scads of extra credit because it is really really hard to do well. Everybody says how smart they are through teeth gritted with envy, which is second only to boatloads of money as the novelist's greatest reward.

If you insist on going this route, betting double or nothing, there is nothing we can say to help. All we can do is let you get back to work. For you, there is no point in reading the next section.

PART VII

HOW NOT TO SELL A NOVEL

What's that? Despite all our time and effort, you've written a publishable novel? No, we're not angry. We're just disappointed. Disappointed and hurt.

But never fear! Your novel is still a long way from ever seeing the light of print. Because, if you play your cards right, the query letter is *the only page of your writing anyone will ever read*.

Remember, editors and agents are very busy people, and all they need is one good reason to shovel another manuscript from the slush pile into the "not my problem" pile.

Give them that excuse! Perhaps you have some grievances against the world of publishing you'd like to get off your chest? What better place to express those feelings than a letter going straight to publishing professionals? Or perhaps you have some grave last-minute doubts about the plotting of your book? Be sure to point them out in the query letter.

But what if the editor or agent is so busy that she won't read the query letter at all? Then where will you be?

Relax! You've still got the synopsis. Use this to painstakingly list the events of the book without the slightest regard for how they relate to the plot. With this single technique, *The Silence of the Lambs* can be made to seem like a formless grab bag of entomology, transvestism, Appalachian poverty, haute cuisine, and sewing instructions, with a hostage situation thrown in to spice things up.

But if you have real panache, no matter how good the writing is, it can be overcome by simply misspelling every other word. Or set aside a weekend to reformat the manuscript in 9-point type in a variety of fun fonts, one for each character.

We know you've worked long and hard to get here, but take a deep breath and go the last few yards. In this final section, you will learn how to ensure that no matter how beautifully you write, nobody need ever find out.

THE QUERY LETTER

Dear Sir or Ma'am:
I know you're very busy, but I hope you'll excuse my daring to send you my first probably pitiful attempt at a novel. I'm fully aware that my English is no great shakes, and the plot isn't perfect (I think the whole first 100 pages could be cut, actually) and probably the main character isn't that likable, because she's based on me. I also would like to offer to forego any advance, 'cause I only want money if the novel actually sells. In fact, if it helps, you can keep all the royalties, too. I can just take a second job . . .

This sort of approach might work for you in your day-to-day life, but . . . actually, it's not working for you there, either, is it?

Even if your general tone is not this spineless, watch out for the apologies and attempts to forestall criticism that can creep into query letters. The time to focus on your novel's flaws is when you're revising it, not when you're pitching it.

> Dear Mr. Hot-shot Agent Guy,
> What are the chances? Some guy writes to you from itsy-bitsy Rhode Island, the Armpit of America (don't ask what it smells like! I'll give you a hint—P.U.!) and tells you his novel is the best thing since sliced lawyers. Only, this time, IT'S TRUE!!! I can see you're shaking your big head with its giant literarily brilliant brain (flattery will get me everywhere, right? LOL). But take one look at *Murder Most Fowler*, the amazing tale of Norman Fowler, the slapstick sleuth, and you'll be laughing out of the other side of your checkbook—guaranteed!

The query letter is a business letter. An agent or an editor who agrees to work with you will want to know that you take a professional attitude to your writing, because it is the way they make their money. You don't have to be completely impersonal, and there's nothing wrong with a little humor, but just as it would show poor judgment to wear an "I'm With Stupid" T-shirt to a job interview, you should not fill your query letter with wisecracks.

> Dear Editor:
> . . . so when I got out of the Army, which is another long story (I'll get to that in a minute) and before I began my career as a waterfront orchid farmer and lost everything in El Niño—an experience I'll never forget unless I suc-

cumb to the Alzheimer's disease that has consigned my father, my paternal uncle, and my friend Willy to residential care homes—it was then that I first came up with the idea for *So Many, Many, Many Ways of Saying the Very Long Thing I Can't Remember Anymore, Lucille*. And, as I alluded to on page 7 of this letter, and went into in slightly more detail on page 11 . . .

Please be concise.

To Whom It May Concern:
Enclosed please find my 200,000 word science fiction novel *One Glorious, Valiant Foe*, in which Kirk and McCoy team up with Han Solo and Chewbacca . . .

Okay, stop right there. Sorry you didn't mention this 200,000 words ago. You're not allowed to use other people's copyrighted characters. You can usually get away with it in fan fiction, if you're just going to post it or share it with your friends, but as soon as there is even the hint of a suggestion of the possibility of money being involved, their lawyers will sniff you out and crush you like a grape. Chances are that if you are so familiar with these characters that you went and wrote a novel about them, the copyright belongs to a huge, impersonal corporation, and it keeps phalanxes of lawyers busy day and night to ensure that nobody uses their intellectual property without permission.

Whenever you see novels published using somebody else's characters, it was prearranged by the copyright holder.

Now go back and change all the names.

Dear Editor:

. . . and so if you can sign and return this nondisclosure agreement, I will send you my novel, but you also have to promise not to show it to anybody . . .

Unpublished authors tend to be more concerned than published authors about the possibility that somebody might steal their ideas. This is because published authors know that there is no end of ideas, and what you're selling is largely in the execution. It is very different from the film business, where a story idea alone is a property, which may be sold separately from a script. Yes, a clever, original plot with an irresistible hook is a great place to start, but there is a remarkably low incidence of plot thievery in professional publishing. Nobody you should be sending your novel to is going to steal your plot.

Dear Editor-in-Chief of a Major Publishing House:

. . . and you're lucky I'm giving you the chance to publish my novel. I can assure you it will be a feather in your cap when I collect my Academy Award for novel, because I will probably thank you in my acceptance speech.

I'm a very busy man, and I want to see this book on the shelves six weeks from now, so I can only give you a few days to make the most important decision of your career . . .

Confidence is generally helpful in business, but all you will achieve by swaggering in a query letter is to make the editor actually *enjoy* crushing you.

As an unknown, unpublished novelist you are like a person applying for an entry-level job at a major corporation. Just as you would not send Bill Gates a resume and a cover letter saying that his piss-ant business will go under without your timely help, it is best not to take a high-handed attitude when submitting a novel.

> Dear Mr. Perkins:
> . . . people in my writing group have compared me to a cross between Thomas Pynchon and Beatrix Potter; others have been reminded of both Tom Wolfe and Thomas Wolfe; I myself think my writing is most like that of my two greatest influences, H.P. Lovecraft and Jackie Collins . . .

The purpose of comparing your work with that of well-known writers is to allow potential buyers of your manuscript to categorize your novel. Do not go into the various subtleties of influence, because nobody is interested. Also do not lean too heavily on any supposed similarity between your work and James Joyce's, because nobody is going to take your word for it.

Also, if you use compound comparisons, try to use writers who can be put together without making anybody's brain hurt.

> Dear Anyone:
> While writing this novel, I've gone through a very painful divorce, which opened a channel in me to the heart of the strugglings of the Modern Male. This book came literally flooding out of me in the course of just eight months, in a process I couldn't control. It was a time when I was moving around a lot, which I think you can see in the

way varied settings are such a feature. Finally, I should
mention that the "seeping potato eye" rash that afflicts
my character in the latter part of the novel is something
I, along with hundreds of thousands of other Dutch-
Americans, have long suffered in silence, but no longer . . .

Writing a novel is a very personal experience, but selling a novel
is business. If details of your life are uniquely relevant to the
marketing of your novel—you were a Navy SEAL, and you've
written a novel about Navy SEALs, say—you should certainly
mention them. Otherwise, the time to share is when the agent
or editor asks you to.

Dear Harlequin Books:
. . . also, I think this book would make a great movie, with
maybe Brad Pitt in the role of Steele, and Jessica Alba
as Lindanna-lou. When my trilogy is written, that could
mean *Love's Lingering Lumbago* II, III, and—who knows
where the triumph could end? I have already picked out
the perfect outfit to wear on Oprah . . .

Fantasize away; everybody does it. Exercise discretion in sharing
those fantasies, though. Carts and horses work best when placed
in the traditional order.

Dear Editor:
. . . and with the second chapter almost entirely in hand,
I expect to have the rest of the book nearly done before
the end of the '08–'09 lacrosse season.

Novels can take a long time to write. At some point during the writing of your novel, you might read of other novels similar to yours being published, events in the news that are key to your plot might resolve or change, or you might just be wracked with anxiety and fear that the world is passing you by. What with the Internet and all, will there even be novels by the time you're done?

Relax, take a deep breath, and get back to work. While it is possible to sell genre novels with a few chapters and an outline, first-time novelists are almost always better advised to finish the book first. See "When to Propose" below.

When to Propose

If you do not have a solid track record as a writer already, you are extremely unlikely to convince an editor to buy your unfinished manuscript. Remember that your competition includes many other novels that are finished. You would have to give an editor an awfully good reason to spend her money on half a novel when she can buy a whole one with the same money, and know exactly what she's getting.

What counts as a "solid track record"? This will vary from case to case. If you have published a book before, this will make all the difference, even if that book is non-fiction. If you have been working as a journalist for years, that will also impress editors. But if your track record consists of writing band reviews for a friend's blog, you probably shouldn't start borrowing against your advance yet. Copywriting is usually not enough, either. While the press releases you've been writing for the Fish Preservative Marketing Board may well be catchy and cogent, and even add up to several weighty tomes—well, life isn't fair.

Of course, the best way to sell a book on a "partial"—or sell a book at all, for that matter—is when the editor is your sophomore roommate from Yale (see "life isn't fair," above).

If you *are* in a position to pitch a book without having a complete manuscript, you will need to submit

- a query letter, including a quick engaging explanation of the book, its market, and your credentials
- the first few chapters of the book
- a synopsis, including a *thorough* outline of the rest

Note that even though you haven't finished the book, you will have to demonstrate that you know how it ends.

But what if you change your mind later and decide that Margana survives being swallowed by Digesto and goes on to find love with St. Diego, the defrocked Franciscan anagram? Well, there are limits to how much can change. You should not pitch a horror novel, for instance, and then deliver a tender coming-of-age story. But don't sweat the details; as long as the outline is a great story and the eventual book is a great story, things shouldn't go too badly.

THE SYNOPSIS

Do Not Include the Dog-Washing Scene

Chapter Three. John comes home and realizes that Fluffy (the Doberman pinscher he got from a rescue group in New Jersey when he was still going out with the eponymously named Fluffy, a stripper) needs a bath. Since he only has five dollars in his pocket, and the dog-washer charges seven (ironic because he spent two dollars on the magazine his ball-busting sister then didn't even want!), he'll wash Fluffy himself. He wrestles with Fluffy humorously.

Meanwhile, the sun is beginning to set, which is beautifully described the way John witnesses it through the bay windows overlooking . . .

Do not include the dog-washing scene.

Also, don't include all those other scenes that don't contain any plot. The synopsis should be shorter than the novel—and not just by five pages.

The Reading Group Guide

In Chapter Three I introduce the image of the snake (masculinity, the Eden myth, shedding skin = regeneration) opposed to the image of Lindanna-lou's torn underpants (violation, the Rape of the South, the specter of Third Wave feminism) to create a richly nuanced fabric of signification. (This is NOT Freudian, but based instead on a combination of R.D. Laing–inflected transactional psychology with a Nozick-style libertarian political rhetoric.)

The color blue also comes up repeatedly, alternating with "neutral" chapters where I pointedly avoid color words (an American flag, for instance, is described as "star shapes in a rectangle, and an L-shaped stripey section") to reflect the draining of color from Steele's life during his separation from Sassafras. In general, the structural play of meaningnesses in *Love's Lingering Lumbago* is the main "action". . .

Nobody has ever been compelled to turn the page out of a burning desire to find out what imagery the author uses to represent impotence or longing. This approach produces synopses that are actually *longer* than the novel, or feel that way.

Just the facts, ma'am.

The Cliffhanger

And this all builds to an amazing surprise climax, full of twists that reveal things about Blade, Steele, and Prong that Sassy could never have imagined! Stunning, surprising things! Things that will turn her world upside down in ways that will thrill the reader to the core of her being.

But to tell any more would be to ruin the ending. . . .

Did we mention that this is a business?

People who are considering purchasing your book want to know how the story ends, up front. You will not be "ruining it"; you will be giving them crucial information they need to make a decision.

PRESENTATION

"Spellcheck" Isn't in My Dictionary

John woak up, in his Master bedroom and, begun to stroak his beatifull dobermin pincer "Fluffy". "Fluffy" barked a littel bit wrigling rond and puting his pointey "nose" intoo John's face and his paw's on the clean cleen bed while, John batted him away laughign, all-the whial.

Some manuscripts end up looking like the label on a bottle of Dr. Bronner's. This doesn't just happen to the manuscripts of writers with abysmal spelling and punctuation skills; it is often because an author hasn't bothered to correct all the typos.

You have to correct all the typos.

Surprise Quiz

How many of the typos do you have to correct?
1. None of the typos
2. Some of the typos
3. All of the typos

Many beginning writers say, "But publishers have copy editors for that! Who cares about those superficial details if the story is really good?"

To which we say: we all want to be loved for our true selves, our inner essence, but that doesn't mean we don't take a shower and look in the mirror before we go out on a date.

If you do have substandard spelling and/or punctuation skills, or you think that your manuscript could benefit from a more thorough cleanup by somebody else, don't fool around. Get help *before* you submit your novel. This could be a friend, but if you are the most literate in your immediate circle, consider paying someone.

FORMATTING

Unlike writing a novel, formatting a novel for submission should not involve any creativity. Therefore, just this once, we'll skip the How Not To, and tell you what to do. You cannot go wrong with the following:

One-inch margins, double-spaced, 12-point Times New Roman (or something else that does not call attention to itself, like Courier).

Number your pages sequentially—that is, do not start from 1 at the beginning of each chapter.

Print on only one side of the page.

Identify the manuscript by putting your last name or the title of the novel in the header along with the page number.

Indent new paragraphs; do not also add another line space between them.

Screenplays are presented in binders; novels are not. Do not bind, staple, or otherwise permanently affix the pages to one another in any way. (A rubber band, though, is helpful.)

Chapter One goes first, Chapter Two goes second, Chapter Three goes third: If you feel that putting your best foot forward requires putting Chapter Seven first, it is time to rethink Chapters One through Six. The reader in the bookstore is not going to pick the book up and jump right to Chapter Seven. If Chapter One is not convincing, the reader will never see Chapter Seven.

WHERE NOT TO SEND YOUR NOVEL

Dear Harvard University Press:
I am writing to submit my blockbuster science fantasy novel, *The Magi of Dorm,* which I think would be an interesting departure from your usual academic emphasis . . .

Send literary works to literary publishers; popular works to popular publishers. No mass market science-fiction publisher is going to be tempted to purchase your Joycean *tour de force*; likewise, literary publishers are not going to see the deeper meaning of your swords-and-sorcery book. To a certain degree, the same goes for agents. Though many agents are willing to try new things, they do specialize, and any good guide to agents will offer lists of genres that an agent wants to handle.

> **Dear Agent Who Specified "Query Letter Only":**
> **Please find enclosed the 500-page manuscript of my novel**
> *But I'm More Specialer Than Everyone Else* . . .

Do not send your whole manuscript to an agent who specifies "first approach by query letter," "query letter only in first instance," or "no unsolicited manuscripts." All you are achieving by doing this is enriching the people who produce ink cartridges, and ruining the chances that that agent will *ever* read your manuscript.

The query letter, when used correctly, serves everyone's interests. The agent can weed out the crazies and illiterates, and the author can make her novel sound *incredibly, unstoppably* commercial. And when an agent asks to see your novel based on your letter, you can be reasonably sure somebody in the office is actually going to read it.

> **To the Fuxom and Snickers Agency:**
> **Enclosed is the manuscript of my novel that you asked to**
> **read, along with a check to cover the $500 reading fee.**

Agents make their living by selling books, not by reading them. If an agent is charging you a fee to read your book, you would probably do just as well responding to that intriguing e-mail from Nigeria. There are also editors out there who will help you with your novel for a fee, but they range from very good to a complete waste of your time and money, and none of them can guarantee you publication. If they do guarantee you publication, they are not editors; they are either a front for a subsidy press, or they are big fat liars. (For further discussion, see "The Last Box," below.)

Writers' organizations maintain online lists of agents and editors to avoid; be sure to check them before you send anybody any money. Because there is always going to be somebody new trying to take your money, these lists cannot be exhaustive, but you can at least eliminate the most notorious of them.

The Last Box

Call us old-fashioned, but we believe that money should travel in only one direction—*from* the publisher *to* the writer. In fact, though we said that there would be no rules in this book, we will now, at the last possible moment, propose one:

Rule #1: The novelist strives at all times to get paid.

This would seem to take self-publishing through a subsidy press, or vanity press, off the table, but we also recognize that the world of publishing—and the world, for that matter—is in constant flux, and that traditional publishing is no longer the only valid model.

For one thing, vanity is no longer considered a vice; it now blends seamlessly into self-esteem, self-confidence, and self-promotion. In some careers, it is part of the job description. Furthermore, the Internet has changed the publishing equation through the ability to reach niche markets, the viability of print-on-demand, alternate channels of distribution, etc.

Lately, these changed circumstances have led to some impressive success stories involving subsidy presses and self-published authors. Note, though, that success in all these stories is signified by the fact that the author, having gone it alone, propelled only by self-esteem, self-confidence, and self-promotion, is offered a book deal by a traditional mainstream press.

The process of trying to sell your novel begins with an act of submission, and it can go steadily downhill from there. The barrage of rejection slips that follows can ultimately take its toll. All in all, it has the potential to become remarkably close to no fun at all.

So, while we believe that the reading public continues to be well served by an editorial selection process, and we believe that when the author opts out of it something very important is lost, we understand that you might feel otherwise. We won't argue; you might well be right. We will not even raise the question of whether or not that makes you a published author. We hope, though, that if you choose that route and turn to people who would publish your 600-page shopping list and tell you you're a genius, you will not also abandon your responsibility to write the best novel it is in your ability to write (see above, pp. 1–254).

AFTERWORD

Congratulations! If you have been following along, you should now have progressed from being merely an unpublished novelist to being a novelist who is completely invulnerable to publication. Clad in the armor of incomprehensibility and offensiveness, you can laugh at the threat of publication! You can sleep at night secure in the knowledge that not a single soul you are not related to by blood, marriage, or fraternal bond will ever read your work, let alone publish it.

You could hold both Harper *and* Collins hostage without a chance of their employees ever agreeing to print a book on which your name appears. If Mr. Random were desperate to sleep with you, Mr. House would still step in and make sure he did not publish your novel. You could be a full-blooded Norseman—Eric the Red himself—and the editors of the Viking Press would still rather set off for Valhalla in a flaming longship than publish you.

Etc.

And now, free from any threat of scrutiny by readers, you will be able to fully develop the majesty of your natural voice. The sacred true-ness of your visioning will never be sullied by the grimy paws of commerce.

We hope that you have come to see us as more than writing-manual hacks; we hope that we have been your liberators—the Spartacuseses, the Che Guevarae, of writing-manual hacks.

However, if you have perversely refused to use the lessons

offered in this book as we intended, and instead avoided each of the mistakes we describe, perhaps you now find yourself a published author. In that case, our follow-up book, *How Not to Make a Living Wage*, will be indispensable. We offer step-by-step instructions in how to steal toilet paper from public restrooms; we revive the lost Depression-era art of subsisting on free ketchup and sugar packets; and we list the very best tactics for borrowing money on a first date. Attempting to live on the advances paid by publishers, you will find our chapter on which cardboard boxes are best suited to your state's specific climate a real life-saver.

But whichever path you choose, the lonely high road of the unpublished or the craven compromised path of the in-print, our good wishes go with you.

Vaya con Pollo! Arroz con Dios! We wash our hands of you! Or, as our parents said to us as they sent us off to college, "We are sorry to inform you that your manuscript does not suit our needs at the present time."

INDEX